Artisan
Edinburgh

CATHERINE AITKEN

Artisan
Edinburgh

CATHERINE AITKEN

The author, Catherine Aitken, at work in her studio in Coburg House Studios in Leith, Edinburgh, where she successfully combines heritage cloths with contemporary design.

First published 2019

The History Press
97 St George's Place
Cheltenham
GL50 3QB
www.thehistorypress.co.uk

British Library Cataloguing in Publication Data.
A catalogue record for this book is available from the British Library.

ISBN 978 0 7509 8935 0

Design by Jemma Cox
Printed in China

MIX
Paper from
responsible sources
FSC® C020056
FSC
www.fsc.org

Contents

Acknowledgements

First, I'd like to thank all the artisans featured in this book. They were so generous with their time, and it was a joy to learn about all the very different approaches to creativity and craftsmanship they were willing to share with me when I visited their studios and workshops for the book. I'm also grateful to the many artist friends and colleagues who have been supportive of the project – there's a wealth of talent in Edinburgh and this book could easily have been twice the size – I wish I could have included many more.

Practical contributions and help came from my sisters Margaret Aitken and Janet Begg; their support and advice was, as always, very much appreciated. A special thank you must go to Juanita Hall at The History Press for having the confidence to commission me to write this book and set me on this very enjoyable and educational path. And finally, a huge thank you to all my family and friends who have been continually supportive right through this process, especially to my friend Annelene Hursthouse.

Catherine Aitken, 2019

About the Author

Catherine Aitken is a designer/maker based at Coburg House Studios in Leith, Edinburgh. Working mostly with Scotland's heritage cloths of Harris Tweed, waxed cottons and linens, she creates accessories for men and women, all handcrafted in her studio. The range of backpacks, handbags, messenger bags and more are often teamed with Scottish deerskin and Italian leather. The designs are functional, with a contemporary fashion twist that combines trend with tradition.

Catherine had a previous career as a producer in film and TV drama and documentary before setting up her eponymous label, working in both creative industries for a while before deciding to concentrate on working as a designer/maker full time. Film is still one of her main inspirations though, and the style and names of the individual designs reflects that.

The collection can be found at her online shop and is also stocked at the V&A Dundee, the British Museum and various boutiques and galleries throughout the UK. Special commissions have included collections with tennis coach Judy Murray (available at Andy Murray's Cromlix Hotel) and for the National Galleries of Scotland and Glenfiddich. Catherine has also taken part in events and exhibitions such as the Craft Scotland Summer Show, Handmade Britain, and #Glow18; and was selected to exhibit at the American Craft Council Baltimore Show under the Craft Scotland banner.

www.catherineaitken.com
www.facebook.com/CatherineAitkenStudio
Instagram: @catherinaitken
Twitter: @catherinaitken

Introduction

Edinburgh is a beautiful city. The capital of Scotland since the fifteenth century, it's a UNESCO World Heritage site, ranking alongside the likes of the Taj Mahal in importance architecturally. Edinburgh Castle dominates the skyline and Princes Street Gardens and Waverley Station sit perfectly between the Georgian splendour of the New Town and the medieval Old Town. Locals and tourists alike love wandering through the city streets, enjoying the architecture, the cobbled streets and the cosmopolitan atmosphere.

The city also boasts many art galleries, both public and private: The Scottish National Gallery; The Scottish Portrait Gallery; The Scottish National Gallery of Modern Art; The City Arts Centre; The Fruitmarket Gallery; The Ingleby Gallery; The Open Eye Gallery – it's a very long list with far too many on it to mention here. The diversity of art one can see, on any day of the week, enriches our society and brings visitors from all over the world to enjoy it. We can also see art in public spaces: Sir Eduardo Paolozzi's *Manuscript of Monte Cassino* comprising a sculpture in bronze of a giant foot and matching hand and ankle. The spectacular *First Conundrum*, by Remco de Fouw, was inspired by Neolithic stones found in Scotland. You can find many examples of the original Neolithic stones in the National Museum of Scotland. No one really knows what these stones were used for but the 5,000-year-old artistic skill is evident.

Two minutes from the city centre we can visit the Mansfield Traquair Centre to see the stunning murals created by Phoebe Anna Traquair in the 1890s. On the outskirts of the city is

Jupiter Artland, a contemporary sculpture park in West Lothian. The stunning *Little Sparta*, the garden of Ian Hamilton Finlay, is in the Pentlands. For the lucky Edinburgh citizens and visitors, art is everywhere.

Working away alongside the galleries and public artworks is Edinburgh's burgeoning creative community. The city is quite well served with studio spaces across various different neighbourhoods. There's at least ten complexes, with some having space for up to 100 creatives working in a variety of disciplines: textiles, printmaking, ceramics, jewellery, glass artists, furniture makers and more. And there's always the need for more space. The advent of the Internet has made it much easier for artists and designers to show and make a living from their work. Nearly everyone has an online presence, or uses some form of social media as a showcase.

Artisans are also assisted by the presence of Craft Scotland, the national development agency created to support makers and promote craft. Based in Edinburgh, the organisation is at the forefront of helping Scottish craft practitioners run their businesses and exhibit their work. Every August there is the Craft Scotland Summer Show where a select group of Scotland's artisans present their work to the international audience visiting for the festival. The agency also organises showcases in London at Collect and the London Design Festival, as well as co-ordinating attendance at Scotland's Trade Fair and NY Now, the international gift fair in New York.

Besides the Craft Scotland Summer Show there are other opportunities to see handcrafted work. For the last three years Handmade Edinburgh have celebrated the best in high-end design and craftsmanship and hope to do so again at The Royal Botanic Gardens in 2020. The Scottish Gallery continually presents the work of handcrafted ceramics, jewellery and textiles including an exhibition by one of our featured artisans Lara Scobie – *Form & Surface*. The City Arts Centre's aim is to champion historic and contemporary visual and applied arts. It recently acquired work by Frances Priest (also featured in this book) – *Gathering Places/Grammar of Ornament – India i*. #Glow18 was an inaugural show hosted by The Dovecot Gallery and curated by James Donald that concentrated on textiles. The show was such a success that #Glow19 is already booked at the same splendid venue, this time over two weekends in August 2019. Open Studios have also become incredibly successful as more and more people want to see, and buy, handmade from local designer/makers. Nearly all the studio buildings do some form of open day or weekend throughout the year. Coburg House Studios in Leith is a perfect example of the kind of hub that individual artists have created when they come together as a group. The Coburg building is home to over seventy artists of various disciplines including painting, textiles, signwriting, illustrations, jewellery, glass, and ceramics. Twice a year the building opens its doors to the public and nearly 3,000 visitors are welcomed over one weekend. Coburg has opened their gallery space every weekend to host exhibitions by the tenants and other artists who want the opportunity to showcase their work. The front of the gallery has been set up as a shop space, also open every weekend. The Gallery Shop sells the work of the studio tenants, who then take it in turns to run the shop. It's a wonderful example of how those with spaces in a studio complex can work as a community to expand the opportunity of their creative businesses.

Workshops and courses can also be a big part of the craft practitioner's portfolio, offering expertise and skills to people wanting to learn about a particular discipline. It could be for those who dream of a career using their handcrafting skills, or perhaps those who would just like to understand a little bit better how things are produced and have some fun. Teaching is just another example of how studios and workshops can be used to pass on skills to a new generation of artists.

Artisan Edinburgh shows you a little of what is happening inside some of the studios in and around the city. This book would like to celebrate these artists and designer/makers and give an insight into what they have to say about their work. On an everyday level we don't often get to see the work of such highly skilled contemporary artisans. Artisans that exhibit throughout the world and win wonderful awards – what can they tell us about what it took to get to this point in their careers?

We all admire craftsmanship, finding delight in handmade objects – whether they are functional, or art, or both. But how are they made? What techniques and processes does it take to make objects so beautiful they can make us quite dizzy with delight when we look closely? What is the thinking behind the design of a vessel, or a piece of furniture, that we may have purchased to enhance our living space? Every time we see or touch these wonderful handcrafted things, we can admire the artistry and dexterity, but what are the processes involved in creating them? The artisans of this book have very generously given us a little insight into their studio lives, to tell us about their creativity and give us an understanding of how they work.

This book profiles the work of twenty-four highly skilled artisans across a variety of disciplines, and within each discipline there is an exciting diversity of materials and methods. For example, the jewellers featured create their work in resin, enamel, ceramics and/or precious metals. The textile designers include specialities in quilting, screen-printing, weaving, kiltmaking and fashion design. The artisans also share with us their backgrounds: how did they get to where they are today? Did they have to study and if so, where? When did they know they wanted to follow a creative path?

The designer/makers in the book discuss their materials, tools and their methods. They also share their inspirations, telling us where they might go to see work that influences them. The National Museum of Scotland is often cited in the book as an excellent source and if you've already visited, you'll know this is not at all surprising. The varied collections encompass history, art, design, fashion, science and technology – from Scotland and throughout the world.

These talented artisans are all very experienced and successful in their chosen fields. A common thread from those featured is how happy they are that their skilful craftsmanship continues to allow them to do what they love to do – that is what they are most proud of. I hope you too are inspired by the individual stories and stunning work that is showcased in *Artisan Edinburgh*.

Kaz Robertson

JEWELLERY DESIGNER/MAKER

Kaz Robertson's workspace is part of a converted warehouse that contains a warren of different sized studios over four floors in the Leith area of Edinburgh. The space is on the top floor and is reached via a final steep flight of narrow stairs with encouraging messages drawn into the stair risers, a leftover from a recent Open Studios event, encouraging visitors to 'just come a bit further', 'not far to go now', and 'check out what we've got!' Little messages for visitors that give a sense of the community, industry and talent in Coburg House Studios. Straight ahead at the top of the stairs, we move into a light and bright space with combed ceilings and a generous attic window that beautifully reflects the weather of the moment – today it's sunny.

Kaz shares this space with another jeweller and her half of the studio has different areas for making and finishing, arranging work for photography and packaging – where the finished pieces are presented in bright pink branded gift boxes, ready for the lucky new owner to pull out and wear. There's a wall of inspiration which is an eye-catching collage of colour and pattern, and images of her beloved cats.

Initially Kaz had thought about studying woodwork, interested in creating furniture when she first went to Edinburgh College of Art (ECA). 'Luckily, in the first year of our course you didn't have to specialise and could dip into a few different disciplines. I quickly realised that furniture design was not for me but I did love the jewellery department. There was so much you could do in the workshops with different materials and scale – I had never really experienced

contemporary jewellery before this point and once I started working with resin I was hooked and never looked back.'

Kaz's jewellery collection is created entirely from resin. It's a time-consuming process: mould making; mixing pigments; filing; adding marks, stripes and patterns; a lot of sanding and then adding the findings. However, it's all worth it for the dazzling end results that can be achieved – pieces which have wonderful tones and hues, with bold patterns and are tactile and playful.

Kaz explains the laborious but rewarding process: 'The resin comes in a clear liquid and a catalyst is added. It starts setting within ten to fifteen minutes, so you have to work quickly. Occasionally I do leave the resin clear, but I'm obsessed with colour and pattern and these two elements are the main features of my collection. Initially I will have created resin sheets and then from that I can cut, file and sand the materials into the desired forms. I can then create moulds from the shapes that I like – imperfect ovals and circles, unusual shapes with soft edges.'

The resin sets overnight in a specially created 'fume cabinet'. Once the resin is hardened it can be sanded, drilled or sawn and that's how the pattern is achieved – by inlaying the next colour in the grooves or dots to create stripes and spots, or any other decoration that's desired.

There's a little snug room off the studio where all the dirty work is done, resin mixing and sanding for instance, leaving the main studio clear for other less messy work.

The silicone moulds can be used again and again to create more designs or if it's a special one-off order for a client, then a new sheet of resin is produced and the bespoke shapes hand formed for the commissioned work.

As is often the case when making or learning a new skill, initial mistakes can become an exciting and inspiring element that defines a style. While still studying at ECA, Kaz was trying to layer the resin with translucent on top of opaque. Lots of annoying bubbles would appear and would normally be removed as part of the process but she decided to work with this development and the resulting spots are now an identifying element in her work. Sometimes pigment mixing might not go as intended but this can also bring out appealing new colour palettes that wouldn't have been used otherwise. 'I want the customer to enjoy wearing my jewellery and appreciate the little extra details I incorporate. For instance, some pieces are reversible for an added surprise. Others have magnets set within which allows bangles to stick together in sets, or ring tops to be swapped. Mis-matching is another strong element of my jewellery, adding to the unique feeling of my pieces.'

This original and fun collection consists of Wangle Bangles – created in purposely asymmetrical circles in solid colour teamed with translucent and spots. The necklaces range from the Big Hoop, a single 1960s-inspired shape, to Bubble Hoop, a series of smaller circles co-joined to create a layered look, and on to the Cluster Pendants – a group of small cube-like shapes formed tightly together. There are also Don't Match Studs, Square Rings and Cufflinks. The delicious tones of pink, lime green, yellow and orange are bright and popping and are coordinated wonderfully with ivories, charcoals, blacks and maroons. The findings, fittings and chains are silver and oxidised silver completing a charming collection of original limited edition wearable works of art.

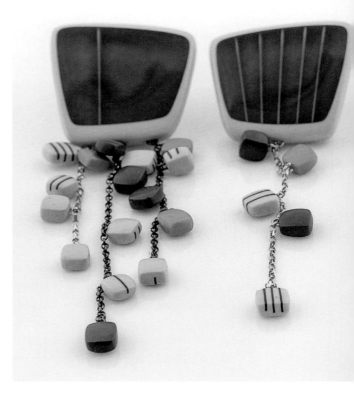

Resin jewellery came to the fore in fashion in the 1960s, complementing the work of designers like Barbara Hulanicki and Mary Quant with their bold, brash colour and shape concepts. It's been popular ever since, still embodying a little bit of 1960s rebellion for the modern admirer and Kaz Robertson's work encapsulates these elements perfectly. As labour-intensive as working with precious metals is, skilfully handmade using the same tools and processes, the collection is tactile, surprising and highly desirable. 'Resin is a fairly cheap material to buy but the working process to get the finish that I require takes a lot of time and effort. I·have found a few shortcuts down the years but I mainly still do a lot of the finishing by hand. I do actually find the finishing quite therapeutic though, which is maybe just as well.'

Modern technology hasn't changed the work process that much. Traditional hand tools are still used all the time. Electric sanders and tumbling machines have speeded up the finishing time but all of Kaz's work has a large element of hand finishing as she hasn't yet found a machine finish she's entirely happy with. There's also a real joy actually working with the material and this is when the process is at its most satisfying, when it's nearly finished and one can see how the different facets are working together. 'Interaction and versatility are two of the most important

aspects of my work. I like the wearer to be able to play with my jewellery, creating new pieces by adding an alternative coloured ring top, or changing around the ear studs. Colour is also an essential element. Layering translucent resin over opaque helps achieves a richer finish and a wider colour range. By patterning either one or both layers I can produce diverse effects.'

'Interaction and versatility are two of the most important aspects of my work. I like the wearer to be able to play with my jewellery, creating new pieces by adding an alternative coloured ring top, or changing around the ear studs.'

For this award-winning jeweller, inspiration comes in many forms. 'Edinburgh is a very pretty city to live in and we are quite spoiled with galleries and exhibitions. On the outskirts of Edinburgh, we have Jupiter Artland. It's a brilliant outdoor sculpture park where you can be surprised by coming upon these works while wandering along the forest walks. And I like a bit of kitsch, so a rummage in a good charity shop or flea market can be a great place of inspiration for me.'

Kaz also has a keen eye for finding random shapes and pattern in architecture and in the bridges and buildings of the local area of Leith. She will quickly snap away when something catches her eye, and often only later will realise that these almost forgotten images have informed a new design.

Kaz has been selected for prestigious shows like SOFA in Chicago and COLLECT and LOOT in New York, as well as being a constant exhibitor at DAZZLE in London and in Edinburgh. The proximity of other designer/makers and artists is also an influence, with the sharing of information about shows and exhibitions a motivation and inspiration for a change in direction or for the creation of new ranges.

Kaz Robertson's adventurous and colourful collections can be found on her own online shop and in the Coburg Gallery Shop. Her work is also stocked in galleries and boutiques throughout the UK and in the US.

www.kazrobertson.com
www.facebook.com/kazrobertsonjewellery
Instagram: @kazrobertsonjewellery
Twitter: @kazrobertson1

Judy R. Clark

WOMENSWEAR FASHION DESIGNER

Award-winning designer Judy R. Clark is famed for her exquisite hand-tailored womenswear designs comprising Harris Tweeds, Scottish lace and antique fabric.

Tipped at an early stage in her career as one to watch by *British Vogue*, Judy has carved a very credible name for herself in the fashion industry, designing womenswear pieces with an eccentric edge in her signature tailoring. The designer has created installations, exhibitions and bespoke ranges for several companies, resulting in a series of prestigious accolades for her innovative and creative approach to fashion design.

Judy always had a love of art and fashion illustration right through childhood and school, so when it came to further education Judy knew she wanted to be able to create three dimensionally the pieces she was designing on paper. Keen to learn all the different disciplines of making and design that weren't available to her at home in Fort William, she successfully applied for a place at Heriot-Watt University and joined the Fashion Design for Industry course with a scholarship to study in the Scottish Borders at just 17. 'We studied knit, weave, print design and garment construction. It was a fantastic underpinning for any designer's career.'

When Judy first arrived on the course, she didn't have any experience of sewing. Although life had been very creative around the kitchen table and at art classes in school, it didn't involve working with fabric that way at all. Initially, the practical making side of the course was the most difficult for her, but she put in the hours, practicing as much as she could and by the time the course ended, was an extremely polished seamstress.

Completing the course with a First Class Honours Degree, Judy then interned under the late and great designer Alexander McQueen. Straight from university and seeing how a successful fashion house worked was a real eye-opener for Judy. The studio was extremely organised with brilliant attention to detail: one of the jobs she remembers well was how immaculately precise the pins needed to be in the pincushions, all colour coordinated and set in a particular way and on Fridays at the end of the day, the interns would sit around the table making sure they were all in the right place.

Once the internship was completed, Judy was eager to set up a fashion label and bring her own designs to life. Returning to Edinburgh, she was successful in securing a grant and business support from local government, which meant she could immediately start working on her first collection.

Her grandmother had introduced her to Harris Tweed by giving her a large suitcase full of the luxury cloth and she chose this cloth as the basis for the new work. Harris Tweed is a beautiful and intricate fabric that's handwoven by islanders at their homes in the Outer Hebrides of Scotland. Created from pure virgin wool dyed and spun in the Outer Hebrides, it's also finished there – and it's the only cloth to be protected by an Act of Parliament. The first collection comprised of short tailored jackets, teamed with lace and silks, in bright colours that resolutely said fashion rather than tradition. Harris Tweed Hebrides, one of the mills on Harris and Lewis, got in touch when they saw the glamorous images she had created for the collection and wanted to use them in a campaign, placing her designs in front of a large audience. Judy was using the fabric in a fresh, feminine and romantic way and with this early recognition of her work, things began to gather pace from there.

Judy's design process is very organic, involving draping. Draping is the art of using fabric to create a design directly on a mannequin. This is an essential skill for fashion designers and a skill that Judy really enjoys and probably uses more than other designers. From pinning, trimming and clipping, and creating shape using darts and tucks, to adding volume using pleats and gathers, and handling complex curves – all is done on the mannequin. 'The designing process is most enjoyable right at the beginning when cloth is flying around the studio and new concepts are being conceived.'

'The designing process is most enjoyable right at the beginning when cloth is flying around the studio and new concepts are being conceived.'

Judy loves to pull fabrics and colours from her boxes and get creative. Sometimes sketches can come at the end of a day when a form takes shape and that can inspire new collections. CAD (computer-aided design) is never used and a pattern is only made up if the design is being created for repeats. 'Everything is hand-stitched onto the mannequin so I don't really know what I'm going to get until the end of the day and that's the most exciting way to work.' It's a bit of a brave move, but Judy finds it energising, getting impatient to see what the design will eventually look like.

The Judy R. Clark studio is set in an old Victorian school building just minutes from Edinburgh city centre and the Scottish Parliament. The space is light and airy with floor to ceiling windows and a wooden grey-painted floor. It has a little bit of a New York studio warehouse vibe; industrial meets chic.

The back wall is covered in inspirational images that have been collected over the years. Little trinkets and books adorn the shelves. Underneath the cutting table are boxes of Harris Tweeds that are still a mainstay in her work: velvets, tulles and silks all stored, waiting to be turned into the next creation. It's a wonderful place to welcome new clients where they can see exactly what's involved from the initial concept to final design.

The first Ready to Wear collection was launched at Milan Fashion Week to great acclaim and recognition, bringing Judy international stockists as well as private clients. You can shop the current Ready to Wear collection online but each piece is still handmade to order. There are dresses, shirts and skirts made from a Madras lace which is produced on nineteenth-century lace looms by MYB Textiles, based in Ayrshire. They are the only producer in the world manufacturing patterned lace with original Nottingham lace looms. Frock coats, jackets, waistcoats, and high-waisted cigarette trousers are available too, created from tweeds, tartans, lace and silks, also made to order from the online boutique.

Judy's everyday work is commissions from private clients. In her studio she has one of everything from her portfolio and when a customer comes in, they can pick and choose from

a selection of cloths, colours and finishes, selecting elements they like or requesting bespoke specifications, and then have these incorporated into the chosen pieces.

However, many clients want something designed especially for them from scratch: it could be a coat, a wedding dress or jacket, but it will all begin with draping and be hand-stitched, including complex embroidery and intricate bead work. Towards the end of the process the design will come off the mannequin and be fitted on to the customer for the last few stitches. Judy finds the painstaking work therapeutic and thoroughly enjoys the process.

> 'Everything is hand-stitched onto the mannequin so I don't really know what I'm going to get until the end of the day and that's the most exciting way to work.'

Other commissions have included being championed by Ford to design a dress using car parts to celebrate the company's centennial year. The Radisson Hotel Edinburgh, Levi's and the Scottish singer Emeli Sandé are all clients. New work coming through is a collaboration with MYB Textiles, where she will create a series of sculptural designs made with their new 'smart' textile: a very special lace that will light up using fibre optics that is woven through the cloth. Judy's collection is also part of the prestigious 'TARTAN', hosted by the Kobe Fashion Museum in Hyogo, Japan's only fashion-oriented museum. 'TARTAN' is a two-year touring exhibition celebrating the Japanese love of tartan and how it is used in fashion design.

This unassuming fashion designer has received various awards for her designs and feels they are testament to the hard work and determination needed to run your own independent business. Inspiration and relaxation are found in Edinburgh's art galleries, trips to the Secret Herb Garden, nestling at the foot of the Pentlands, and walks around historic Stockbridge enjoying the charity shops, local market and little boutiques.

The Judy R. Clark label has showcased on the international stage including New York, Tokyo, Russia, Milan and London, as well as numerous platforms around the UK. The products are timeless: stunning avant-garde collections from couture to commercial, with a distinctive signature style that is instantly recognisable.

www.judyrclark.com

www.facebook.com/JudyRClarkFashionPage
Instagram: judyrclark1
Twitter: @judyrclark

Frances Priest

CERAMIC ARTIST

From her Edinburgh studio, Frances Priest creates intricate and colourful ceramic objects that celebrate her fascination for ornament and pattern, using clay as a canvas on which to build richly drawn and layered surfaces of inlaid line, glaze colour and enamel decals.

The studio is just a fifteen-minute walk from the busy city centre and a similar distance from the foot of Arthur's Seat, an extinct volcano which overlooks the entire city, and Frances enjoys this balance. Part of the Out of the Blue Abbeymount Studios complex that sits within an old Victorian school building, her space is south-facing with a mezzanine area which allows her to divide up activities into making and designing areas. She calls it her haven. Although Frances enjoyed being in a shared studio in the past, she finds that the solitude and ability to be completely absorbed is much better for her creativity and productivity. It's also important for contemplation too, being able to just sit and not do anything is difficult if others are nearby. And if it does get a bit quiet sometimes, then being in a studio complex does offer the best of both worlds, as other artists, designers and makers are not far away, and can drop in and visit or meet for a coffee and a chat.

> 'The making process is fairly straightforward but the end result requires considerable time and patience.'

Frances began her artistic career with a foundation course where she was lucky to be tutored by renowned ceramic artist, David Roberts. He was an inspirational teacher and this experience led her to apply to the Ceramic Department at Edinburgh College of Art. On graduating, her work was selected for Talente, a European survey show of craft and design graduates organised by the Handwerkskammer of Munich, so she quickly had to find a studio space and make new work. This, coupled with a part-time job working in the crafts department of the Scottish Gallery in Edinburgh for curator Amanda Game, got her professional life under way. 'Research, experimentation, inspiration, doubt, commitment, production.'

A recent body of Frances' work – 'The Grammar of Ornament – India Series' – has come from looking at the lavish Victorian pattern book it's named after. Published in 1856 by architect Owen Jones, *The Grammar of Ornament* is a luxurious compendium of pattern, motifs and ornaments from around the world in 112 illustrated plates. Frances had this book since childhood and knew she wanted to make something from it but found it challenging to tackle such a seminal piece of work. An opportunity to travel to India arose and this was a chance to focus on that particular section of the book. It was intriguing to see all these motifs from the book in their original settings and also to see how the designs had evolved. The visit also added a strong understanding of how colour works in India as a place, and these two elements coming together gave Frances a way in to create the India Series.

The process begins with drawing out original designs on paper and creating stencils and metal tools that are used to mark out the designs in clay. The stencils are made from graph paper which Frances uses to trace around, or as a plotter for freehand lines drawn with a scalpel. The metal tools are used to impress areas of pattern into the clay. These are made from aluminium tubing that she cuts and forms into specific shapes, or sometimes even her mother's old cake decorating tools! Frances inherited a collection of these odd shapes, used to cut and make sugar flowers, that she adapts to get the exact shape she requires. Frances will make a hand-built vessel form from clay and then, using a combination of stencils, a scalpel and metal tools, the pattern is built up as a drawing on the surface of the clay. This application of marks made by hand means you achieve the vibration that you always get with a handmade object, giving it a distinctive appearance.

The idea is to reference the fact that these are units that are building up – like inlay, mosaic or stitch. The finished vessels look like they're made from small individual objects that have been placed on top of one another, an unintentional *trompe l'oeil* that is accentuated by Frances allowing the pattern to dictate the top edge. To keep the edge traditionally flat would make the object look self-contained, but allowing this development gives a sense of movement in the work, of the possibility of it evolving and changing. It's taking the flat pages of *The Grammar of Ornament* that may depict plasterwork, or textiles, and turning that into a three-dimensional form that has a kind of mobility.

The next part of the process is to add the colour and select the glazes and this can take a long time to get just right. Will the surface be shiny or matte or something in between? Some glazes don't work so well over large surfaces; other glazes can really sparkle if they're next to a matte surface. Frances has a colour palette that she often returns to, always responding to turquoises and corals. The powdery tones used in the most recent series of work came directly from her experience of seeing the colours in India.

'I enjoy seeing a piece head off into the real world, and meeting it again in a new context can allow me to see it properly.'

Working through all the different stages can take a long time, particularly the extensive hours spent creating the decoration, and one piece may take more than a month to complete. Conveying that sense of labour and commitment is important to the work. It's about speaking to the viewer about the sense of absorption and preciousness that's been involved in the creation. 'The making process is fairly straightforward but the end result requires considerable time and patience.'

The scale of the bigger works, and seeing that intensity of pattern making and drawing over such a large scale, pushes them towards a sculptural statement rather than a decorative.

When the work is finished Frances finds that seeing it properly is quite a hard thing to achieve, especially seeing it in the context of all the other pieces that are around in the studio. 'I find the work is only really complete once it has left the studio; I enjoy seeing a piece head off into the real world, and meeting it again in a new context can allow me to see it properly.'

One of the settings outside the studio where Frances can see her latest work is in the National Museum of Scotland (NMS). The NMS already hold an earlier work from 2003 but fifteen years on her work has evolved and changed dramatically. 'Having NMS take a new piece of mine into the permanent collection and decide they want to follow my career and record the change is very thrilling.'

Frances enjoys all the stages of her artistic process: 'The research stage is where the inspiration mostly happens, whether that's visiting a museum, travelling and experiencing new places, or sitting in my studio chair exploring my bookshelf. I enjoy thinking out ideas through drawing and I have lots of objects and test pieces around my studio that I constantly play with and re-arrange. I try to capture the mutable nature of decorative objects in the final works I make, creating pieces out of multiple forms that can be arranged and composed. I also make individual works in series so that I can explore different aspects of an idea and the works can have a conversation with one another.'

She also loves being in the studio in the middle of a project when she's fully absorbed in the making and the thinking. Opening a glaze kiln can be a very enjoyable moment, when all the hard work comes together. Conversely it can also be the most challenging time, where that hard work has not paid off and you have to begin again.

When it's time to leave the studio, Frances enjoys her proximity to Arthur's Seat and Holyrood Park and loves to climb Salisbury Crags to look out over the city and across the Firth of Forth to the Fife coast. It brings a different perspective and can lift her out of work completely.

New work has now taken Frances into the midst of making a decorative tile scheme for the Royal Edinburgh Hospital, commissioned by NHS Lothian Health Foundation. She's developed the work in collaboration with the wonderful specialist tile manufacturers Craven Dunnill Jackfield and this project is now complete and available for all to see.

The artist's work has been exhibited in Homo Faber – Best of Europe at the Fondazione Giorgio Cini in Venice and 2019 brings presentations at COLLECT at the Saatchi Gallery, represented by the independent gallery Cavaliero Finn. There will also be a summer showcase at the Bowes Museum.

'It's nearly twenty years since graduating from Edinburgh College of Art so I think it is fair to say I am proud to have been able to sustain a career over that period of time. I have had many career highlights. These include undertaking a residency at Cove Park, work being added to various national collections, exhibiting work in Tokyo with Crafts Council UK, but I think the project I am most proud of to date is a commission for Atlas Arts, Patterns of Flora – Mapping Seven Raasay Habitats. It was developed collaboratively with Atlas Arts, botanist Stephen Bungard and Raasay House as a permanently sited work which explores and celebrates the habits and plant life of the Scottish Island of Raasay. It's given me a long-term link to that area of Scotland and it is satisfying to know that the work will be there for many years to come.'

'The research stage is where the inspiration mostly happens, whether that's visiting a museum, travelling and experiencing new places, or sitting in my studio chair exploring my bookshelf.'

www.francespriest.co.uk

https://www.facebook.com/PriestFrances
Instagram: @ francesprieststudio
Twitter: @frances_priest

Emily Hogarth

PAPERCUT ILLUSTRATOR

Emily Hogarth is an artist who has a very short commute: from the back door of her house to the studio in the garden is just a few short steps. On entering, we are struck by the beautiful mobiles hanging from the ceiling of clouds, leaves and abstract shapes. There are colourful architectural templates of work for a current project on the shelves and on the walls and worktops are various other examples of Emily's inventive work. The workshop is certainly a wonderful reflection of her motto 'Making the Everyday Magical'. Mary, the Westie dog, is usually sitting happily under the desk and there are drawers full of prints and other stock for galleries and the online shop. Little pieces of paper litter the floor and it feels exactly what it is – a cluttered creative and industrious studio.

Emily began papercutting while studying textiles at Edinburgh College of Art. Rather than go through the process of creating mesh screens and exposing the images of her patterns and designs for screen printing, Emily found it much easier to just hand cut the stencils and use them directly. With paper or card, Emily would draw the design and cut it out – then it was immediately ready to use for printing. She loved this fast result, speeding up the whole process and allowing freedom to experiment more.

'I think it involves quite a lot
of daydreaming and thinking
about designs.'

Exhibiting at New Designers London followed on from graduation and it was while participating in this important event that Emily realised the visiting companies were more interested in the illustrations in her portfolio than the fabrics she displayed. Her work went down so well that she won a New Designer award, generating excellent press coverage that resulted in exciting work opportunities. After this early success, Emily decided to take a Masters in Design at ECA and began really experimenting with her papercutting compositions. 'I think it involves quite a lot of daydreaming and thinking about designs so that when I actually sit down with a piece of paper in front of me the process is quite fast as I have been designing it in my head for a while.'

Amazingly, the designs are no longer drawn out first – just a sheet of paper on the worktop, a marking tool, a scalpel and a clear idea of how to start the design. It's because the designs evolve so much as she works that Emily doesn't like to be too prescriptive and plan very much ahead, so it's not always clear what the finished papercut will look like. Clearly the designer's work speaks for itself as not knowing exactly what may appear in the finished piece is as exciting for the client as it is for her. In her studio, Emily sits with a list of the elements the client would like to see in the artwork beside her, and refers to the list as she works away with the sharp cutting tool. A nearby handy dish of blunt and broken blades gives an indication of how many can be gone through during the process. Sometimes pieces take a long time and she'll listen to an audiobook or have the radio on in the background as the work proceeds and transforms from a blank sheet of paper to a unique work of art. While lost in the process of cutting, this is when Emily is most inspired to think about new designs and future work, imagining the children's books that she would like to produce, a new range of prints, or a monoprinting course.

An impressive list of clients have commissioned Emily's work – from the National Museum of Scotland; Cadbury's Flake 'Allure'; the Nivea Pearl and Beauty global campaign as well as magazine covers and designs for Jasper Conran for Debenhams (to name just a few). Most recently she was invited to work on the design of a new central atrium at the 'Sick Kids', as the Royal Hospital for Sick Children in Edinburgh is known locally. For this extensive project an illustrator was needed who could bring all the elements of form, space and furniture together and they approached Emily to create it. The designs will reference many local landmarks including turning Edinburgh Castle into a sleeping dragon. Impressive archways for the space will be decorated with her work by being imposed in resin and then added to the structures.

There will be tabletop games and wall decals – all with Emily's illustrations that have been inspired by her home city and besides the castle will reference other well-known landmarks including the Scott Monument and the Balmoral Clock. It's been a complicated, time-consuming but rewarding project and such a fabulous advert for the designer's work that will be seen by the public and enjoyed by children every day.

Very occasionally Emily accepts private commissions, perhaps for a birthday or a wedding. Wherever the commission comes from, each client has their own story or message to illustrate and it's up to Emily to gather all the pieces of information into a cohesive and stunning design. 'I just can't over-plan it. It often begins as a circle in the middle, then I connect everything out from that, making it grow – basically a very fancy doodle!'

Her skill means that she's never had to stop a papercut and start again. Spelling mistakes can happen, especially when writing back to front, but her expertise means she can be very clever with correcting mistakes. If the blade slips, the design is just altered slightly to allow for that and accommodate it into the design. Clients know they're going to get something very special and trust Emily completely to produce a design that goes way beyond their imagination.

The simplicity of the papercutting technique means that little has changed since originating in China where paper was first invented. Initially an expensive art form because of the cost of the paper, it soon levelled out and spread throughout the world as a creative process open to all. In Britain, Victorian silhouettes were an extremely popular way to record people's likenesses before photos. Hans Christian Andersen's original illustrations were papercuts. The practice is now often seen as folk art, easy to create celebratory decorations for your own home in bunting, paper chains and snowflakes. In the last twenty years or so, artists like Emily have taken the process to new levels of craftsmanship and used more contemporary subject matter in their designs. Emily is now such an expert in her discipline that she's written books on the subject, including *The Crafter's Guide to Papercutting*.

In her own collections, Emily captures the magic of the Scottish landscape and its wildlife, creating a recognisable signature style. Working with papercuts, Emily loves the combination of boldness and delicacy that the form brings to the designs. Through their flexibility they can be stand-alone pieces of art or translated onto a printed medium. There are collections of Emily Hogarth cards, aprons, mugs and tea towels. The future might bring a return to fashion design but also a potential children's clothing line – and a series of one-off screen prints is something Emily has long wanted to do.

'I just can't over-plan it. It often begins as a circle in the middle, then I connect everything out from that, making it grow.'

With three young children and a dog to juggle alongside a busy and successful career, Blackford Hill and Portobello Beach are favourite spots for blustery walks and getting away from it all. The Central Library in Edinburgh is a place where she can share her children's enthusiasm for books and their illustrations, and the whole family (minus Mary the dog!) take advantage of the National Museum of Scotland with its diversity of collections.

Emily is proud of the fact that she is able to make a living from her passion, and feels so lucky to love what she does. It's not easy with young children to find the time for new commissions or think about prospective work. But once the children are asleep, she enjoys being at work in the evening too, cutting away in her own creative bubble in the garden studio and feels really privileged to have that escapism and be able to continue her career as a designer.

For many years Emily had a studio space at Coburg Studios in Leith. When she first moved out, Emily missed the proximity and creative buzz of other artists but now feels less isolated. Coincidentally, there are other artists with garden studios in the same street and it has really become a little community. Social media has also made a tremendous difference to how the business and the popularity of her designs have grown. Her large Instagram following means connections with other artists, potential clients and commissions are worldwide and although she never knows where the next piece of work will come from, she wouldn't have it any other way.

You can find Emily's work on her website, in the Red Door Gallery and Curiouser & Curiouser in Edinburgh, as well as Cambridge Contemporary Crafts and Tayberry Gallery in Perth.

www.emilyhogarth.com

Instagram: @emilyhogarth
Twitter: @emily_hogarth

Elizabeth Jane Campbell

ENAMEL JEWELLER

Jewellery designer and enameller Elizabeth Jane Campbell shares a large studio in Beaverhall Art Studios, not far from Edinburgh city centre. The building is an old chocolate factory and now houses a variety of small businesses and creatives including painters, ceramicists, illustrators, and textile and millinery artists.

Sharing at Beaverhall with another jeweller and a jeweller/silversmith, the three designer/makers all work in very different ways but come together to make a pretty good team in the studio – so important when sharing your creative space. It's large enough for all the necessary machinery and equipment and huge windows let in plenty of daylight. The walls are decorated with postcards and posters from previous exhibitions and there's also a wonderful selection of plants dotted along the windowsill in between personal photographs and little doodles. Elizabeth loves working in this shared environment and in the building as a whole, finding the proximity of other artists in different disciplines exciting. It allows her to step out of her own medium and trade different work tips or tools and find out what other artists and designer/makers in the building are up to – a constant influence and source of inspiration.

> 'I love being an enameller – I'm proud to be continuing the history of such a wonderful technique.'

From the youngest age, Elizabeth was passionate about jewellery and as a very small child was already experimenting: 'making terrible bead necklaces and bracelets which my poor mum had to wear!' Her granny's grandfather had worked in a jeweller and watch business in Edinburgh and her granny's jewellery box was like an Aladdin's cave: full of huge stones; bead work and enamel pieces. Jewellery was obviously in her genes and she's never looked back. 'While at school I did various evening and summer classes at ECA as I had such an interest in the subject. After studying for a BTEC in Art and Design at Edinburgh's Telford College, I knew for sure jewellery was the direction I wanted to take so I undertook an HNC in Jewellery and Silversmithing at Cardonald College in Glasgow.'

Elizabeth was accepted into Edinburgh College of Art studying jewellery and silversmithing and is now an award-winning jeweller with her work in the permanent collections of the National Museum of Scotland and The Goldsmiths' Company in London. She studied abroad in her third year, taking a semester at Nova Scotia College of Art and Design and it was in Canada that she fell in love with enamelling, a passion that continues today. 'I love being an enameller – I'm proud to be continuing the history of such a wonderful technique.'

Elizabeth is excited by the scale, technical aspect and detail of jewellery and her collections are very much informed by concepts of visual literacy, and specifically, the idea of balance. Elizabeth uses these concepts in their simplest form – using geometric shape, colour and pattern to create beautiful contemporary jewellery. New projects and designs, whether it's for the latest collection for a gallery or exhibition, or a private commission, always begin with an idea that's developed carefully through sketches, collages and samples. Balance is crucial in the process too, tackling each part of a project step by step, as the success of enamelling depends on a careful, systematic approach.

The enamel craft is one of the oldest in jewellery: the earliest known examples are from the thirteenth century BC: rings made from gold with enamel inlays and the skill of making gold cloisonné and champlevé work was practiced all over the Byzantine Empire. Extremely popular in the 1920s, enamel jewellery has had a resurgence of popularity in recent years and now this craft, often seen as a form of art, is in the limelight once more.

The material used to enamel is glass and that comes in either lump or powder form with Elizabeth preferring the powder version. The lumps, when used at all, would need to be ground down with a mortar and pestle after being hammered into small chunks. This method can take a week just to get the powder to the right consistency, and would only be followed when a particular colour, that isn't available in powder, is desired.

The standard base for Elizabeth's enamel is copper and it's used almost like a canvas, with the powder sifted delicately on to the surface with a tiny little sieve. A desk-top kiln is then used to melt the miniscule granules and fuse them onto the metal. Kiln time and heat level depends on the result you want to get from particular colours. High heat and short fire bring different results from a low heat and a longer fire. This is where the skill and experience really come to the fore and Elizabeth loves the romantic alchemy of it. Opening the kiln and taking a piece out, often it's jet black as the colour pigments have gone into shock but as everything cools then the beautiful colours begin to come through and the piece is magically transformed before your eyes. Alchemy indeed.

Once the work is at the right temperature, the enamel is ground away at under water, thinning it down and creating a matt surface exposing some of what's below. This is a favourite stage for the designer as you can stop at any point, depending on how you like the finish that's coming through, the colour complementing the underlying warmth of the copper. Overall it appears to be a simple procedure but one that takes so much skill to get right. All the work is then set in silver, using regular jewellery tools such as standard saws and pliers and following the same expert craftsmanship as any jeweller. 'Sampling is so important. Sometimes you can do something and love how it turns out but if you can't replicate it, then it wasn't skill it was just luck. You have to be able to know how to do it again and again so you work backwards, find out what it was you did differently and work out how that can be brought into the process. That's when you're pushing the art of enamelling forward.'

Decoration and a touch of luxury are added using cloisonné wires: little ribbons of gold or silver that can be inlaid on one surface or on different layers as they are built up. The Elizabeth Jane Campbell range includes brooches, necklaces, earrings and rings in beautiful oranges, yellows and blues, set within precious metals. Elizabeth also creates collections with oxidised silver, gold leaf and sterling silver, but it's the enamelling process that gives her most satisfaction.

A recent commission has been for a red enamel ring that covers the whole hand. This kind of larger and more sculptural work is something that Elizabeth wants to concentrate more on in the future – bringing a 3D element into the designs. Ninety per cent of being a maker is problem solving and it's the constant experimentation with the technical aspects of enamelling that pushes the stimulating development of new directions.

'The best point of the whole process is definitely the moment someone tries on a piece of your jewellery and falls in love with it. The jewellery comes alive when it's worn, and it is so satisfying to see someone light up when they wear your work. That relationship between wearer and jewellery is so special and it really is the ultimate ending to the whole process of making a piece.'

Since graduating Elizabeth has already had many high points in her career: she won the chance to be part of a small team from Edinburgh-based company Hamilton & Inches that designed and worked on a ceremonial mace for a university. She enamelled the head of the mace in a hand-drawn champlevé maple leaf motif – it's still the largest thing she's ever enamelled.

In 2018 she won the Silver Award at Goldsmiths' Craft & Design Council Awards and has now showcased at Goldsmiths' Fair five times. Her work is represented in the Scottish Gallery in Edinburgh and this is where she also likes to visit for inspiration, enjoying the contemporary collections of glass and ceramics available there. Further stimulus can be found living in Leith as she enjoys taking photos of whatever catches her eye, whether it's colours, shapes, graffiti or buildings – all these things and more inspire and inform her designs. Elizabeth's exquisite work can be found in galleries throughout the UK and abroad, and online through her own website.

www.elizabethjcampbell.co.uk
www.facebook.com/ElizabethJaneCampbellJewellery
Instagram: @elizabethjanecampbell
Twitter: @EJCjewellery

James Donald

WEAVER

James studied Textiles at Duncan of Jordanstone College of Art in Dundee, specialising in tapestry, with printmaking and weave as secondary subjects. However, it wasn't until he travelled internationally, post-graduation, and met weavers from other backgrounds and cultures that he really saw the potential of the weaving skills he'd learned in college.

In Australia he was introduced to the work of Jun-ichi Arai, a Japanese weaver renowned for his complex and innovative work. Often three-dimensional in nature, his fabrics appear as undulating landscapes of puckering, crumpling, puffs and pleats and, as varied as they appear, they all share a simplicity of texture that belies their extremely complex manufacturing techniques. This work inspired James to establish his own weave structure rather than using standard designs. This individual cross structure, influenced by a trip to Uist in the Outer Hebrides, combined with the yarn and colour choices he uses, makes James' work quite unique and easily identifiable.

'I like to think I am marrying contemporary technology with a traditional craft that is thousands of years old.'

Based in a large and airy studio at Coburg House Studios in Leith, James works on a computerised 32 shaft Megado. He still has to treadle, beat and throw the shuttle by hand but the computer enables him to store designs and since acquiring the loom in 2000, he now has quite a library of designs which he can revisit, tweak, adjust and adapt as well as sparking and influencing ideas for new designs. Using the computer is also advantageous in that one can jump to a new design at the click of a mouse which does speed things up. A modern invention for an ancient craft – weaving on a loom began around 6000 BCE when humankind ceased to be nomadic and was able to move from hand weaving to using big heavy looms in situ – looms so large that they wouldn't have been possible to transport easily. 'I like to think I am marrying contemporary technology with a traditional craft that is thousands of years old.'

While working away in his notebook, drawing out new weave structures and choosing a colour palette for forthcoming collections, James listens to the radio, usually Radio 2 or 4 if he needs to concentrate but when he's weaving away, which is most often the case, he loves to put on fast dance-based music to keep the tempo of weaving going. Disco is best!

Working under the brand name PickOne, James creates scarves, ties and snoods using mostly Scottish yarns of Shetland wool and lambswool, and also cotton, silk, linen and Merino wool. Treble-cloth structured scarves in linen and lambswool and mercerised cotton, with a rich colour palette and extremely intricate weave mix in with his collections of iPad Covers, pencil cases and pouches that he's had manufactured from his own cloth. The most recent collection is inspired by Mary Quant with washed out, unsaturated colour rather than the brights he's used in previous ranges. The pastel colours remind him of his childhood when his mother and aunts wore the iconic designs that so inspire him today. A new venture has been the manufacture of very smart retro footstools created in collaboration with an upholsterer working with James' own cloth and a woodturner to create the legs – all to James specifications – an exciting new addition to his portfolio of work.

James finds all stages of his process immersive, including the time-consuming and complicated threading of the loom. He enjoys the meditative state that comes with the extreme concentration and repetitive actions of making sure the yarns are all placed properly. The finishing is all done on the premises too, with a washing machine dedicated to the cloths; it's exciting when the cloths are washed, as depending on what cycle has been used they will have different final textures. When it's a new weave structure James may have to try different temperatures before he finds the right finish for the cloth. 'I take great satisfaction from the way cloth grows before you, the fluid movement of one cloth evolving into the next.'

The PickOne studio space is full of character, with carefully chosen objects that have been picked up along the way. A love of period ceramics is obvious, with collections dotted throughout the studio. Lots of vibrant yarn cones are stored on the walls or hanging from the ceiling. Various plants give the space a relaxed and homely vibe and make it a perfect atmosphere to work on all stages of the process. The shelves are full of fascinating books on the subjects of textiles and art generally. Fifties tins and packets are displayed along with the plants and ceramics, various knick-knacks and weaver tools and paraphernalia. 'Seeing ideas develop from initial photography through sketchbook scribbles and marks and then watching it grow on the loom as I weave through these various concepts is alchemy and it never ceases to amaze me.'

It's an alchemy that this weaver finds most illuminating and a motive to further develop and improve on what's gone before. Should he (rarely) find himself in a creative rut, then he takes himself off to the Outer Hebrides or the Shetlands where through observation of the landscape

> 'Seeing ideas develop from initial photography through sketchbook scribbles and marks and then watching it grow on the loom as I weave through these various concepts is alchemy and it never ceases to amaze me.'

and lifestyle, he comes back with new influences and approaches. On a day-to-day basis he revels in being near the shore, close to the studio and home, using the Water of Leith cycle path to get to nearby Dean Village or Warriston cemetery.

Besides his own work, James is also an experienced teacher, having taught at Dundee College for a few years. He's now given that up to run evening and weekend classes from the studio as well as offering the opportunity to have one-to-one tuition with his expertise. The teacher in him loves that level of communication with students.

The weekend class is more about learning the basics of the process, to understand how cloth is made, and the evening class is for the more experienced student who can do their own thing to a certain extent, but will still need some guidance and advice. The teaching is broken down into manageable chunks and students develop quickly over a short period of time. The small looms can be taken home for work to be finished and it's exciting when a student comes in with a finished scarf and then wants to learn more. James sees teaching as one of the highlights of his career, and it's an aspect of his practice that gives him real satisfaction – passing on his skills to a new generation and introducing the craft of weaving. Weave is no longer taught as a subject to students in art colleges and is in danger of disappearing completely as a skill in contemporary design education. Ceramics has almost disappeared as well from the academic landscape and James is passionate about not losing the knowledge and skills of these crafts. He also teaches about the heritage and history of weave and if he can, he wants to influence the craft landscape and keep these traditional skills alive. Great joy is had from the fact that three students of his have gone on to establish their own businesses as weavers.

With fellow textile designer Fiona McIntosh, James runs Concrete Wardrobe – a shop on the edge of Edinburgh New Town that specialises in craft. Selling a broad range of disciplines including jewellery, accessories, textiles, clothing, prints, glass, ceramics and homewares, Concrete Wardrobe focuses on high quality and affordable gifts, must-haves and collectables. Concrete Wardrobe first started as a pop-up in 2000 but quickly became a permanent establishment and one of the first shops to concentrate solely on handmade products.

Weaver, teacher, businessman – as if that's not enough James has also begun curating and organising shows featuring the work of craft practitioners. #Cloth18 was the inaugural event in 2018 and was such a success that #Cloth19 is already booked. Hosted by Dovecot Studios, a tapestry studio and exhibition space in the centre of Edinburgh, this is a show that concentrates solely on the work of textile artists and designers and is the only one of its kind in Scotland. Born from the fact that there are limited opportunities for designer/makers to sell their work, and with an attitude of 'makers doing it for themselves', James also curated Glow, a Christmas show featuring all disciplines and The Ceramics Show is planned for 2019.

PickOne's collections sell directly at various events throughout the UK and at Coburg House Open Studios. He relishes the opportunity to show his scarves, ties and pouches to clients, especially those interested in weave and who can appreciate the skill and expertise evident in his designs. PickOne also supplies wholesale to galleries and shops and has exhibited internationally. The year 2019 sees James' participation in NY Now, the New York gift show that will introduce his work to a new international audience.

This is a designer whose whole life is intertwined with his love of craft. He enjoys the proximity of other artists in the Coburg building; his friends are mostly makers too and his purchasing choices always involve great design and craftsmanship. It's a lifestyle choice, one that he's very proud of still being able to maintain since launching PickOne in 1997.

www.pickone.co.uk

www.facebook.com/PickOneWeaver
Instagram: @pickone
Twitter: @pickoneweaver
Concrete Wardrobe, 50A Broughton Street, Edinburgh, EH1 3SA

Helen Miles

MOSAIC ARTIST

Mosaic artist Helen Miles trained with master craftsmen in Greece who taught using traditional methods with a focus on Byzantine iconography. She later became interested in Roman mosaics and now makes contemporary pieces inspired by ancient designs.

Always interested in pattern, Helen made quilts as a child and had a fascination for finding repeat shapes and forms, identifying visually pleasing arrangements even while helping her father with his dry-stone walling. A career in journalism took her away from this early passion but she found it again, years later, while living in Greece. With two small children and in an unfamiliar environment she had stopped being able to work or interact with the world the same way as she had done in the past. The decision to train as a mosaicist came one day on a beach in Pelion, a dramatic peninsula jutting into the Aegean Sea. 'I was running pebbles through my fingers, savouring their colours and differences, when I realised with blinding certainty that I wanted to make mosaics.' In this moment of epiphany she knew that the stones were not just what she loved, but it was what would release her back into the world again.

From that point on everything changed and she began studying mosaics with master craftspeople in Thessaloniki and Athens. Thessaloniki in particular is celebrated for its world-renowned Byzantine churches, many of which are richly decorated with mosaics. 'I was mesmerized by the painstaking intricacy of the designs as well as the beauty of the materials and resolved to immerse myself in this ancient artistic practice.'

Helen now sees mosaics everywhere and in the everyday. For example, while walking with a friend past a field of corn she showed how that was a mosaic too: 'Mosaics are really nothing but the slow and deliberate accumulation of parts; the materials change, the way of achieving that accumulation changes, but essentially, they all boil down to the same thing – to pattern, line, movement, form.'

This passion that Helen rekindled on a beach in Greece has now turned into a successful business making site-specific mosaics to commission using mostly stone and marble. While her work is inspired by classical designs it is also resolutely contemporary and can be equally applied to walls or floors as well as being hung as panels.

'The process of making a mosaic very much depends on the type of mosaic that I am making – whether it's on site, embedded in an interior space or outside, or for a floor or a wall. I enjoy working on commissions which respond to people's stories leading to works which have an overt (or covert) personal element to them.'

The initial stages of designing a mosaic involve researching and sketching as well as considering the choice of materials – whether it will be in stone or in specialist mosaic materials. Once the design is completed, the mosaic is made off-site in the artist's studio.

Helen's preferred method is working on mesh so that the design is laid out on a board under a plastic film with the mesh layer on top. The stones are fixed to the mesh with glue and then when the work is complete it can be cut into pieces and fitted together on site like a jigsaw. Before fixing, the stones are treated with at least three coats of a specialist sealant which brings out their natural colours and protects them. Finally, the mosaic is fixed to the wall using tile adhesive, just like fixing bathroom tiles, and then grouted. The huge advantage of this method is that the mosaic can be cut up, thus mitigating the difficulties of transporting and installing a large work.

Helen also makes smaller hangable panels on wood or Jackoboard, which is a kind of compressed foam board suitable for outdoors. If the mosaic is for a floor it's made using the reverse method on paper – the stones are placed upside down on brown paper with a water-soluble paste. Again, if it is a large mosaic, the paper can be cut into sections for ease of transportation and installation. On site, a mortar bed is prepared, and the sections are placed into the mortar and then the backing paper is removed by wetting it and peeling it off, revealing the correct side of the mosaic in all its beauty.

Each tessera, or piece of the mosaic (and sometimes a work will contain thousands of tessera) is cut and shaped by hand and laid in a slow and deeply satisfying process, where colour, balance and minute adjustments are constantly being considered. Usually stones are acquired in 1cm thick rods and then cut using a stone cutter – a large, heavy tool permanently fixed to a table. It consists of two blades, one of which is pulled down with a lever to break the stone placed on the lower blade. Once the stone is roughly the right size to work with, slight alterations are made to it by hand using small nippers if needed. Traditionally, mosaicists use a hammer and hardie to cut stone, a tool which has been around since Roman times, so using a stone cutter is slightly cheating but making mosaics is a long and time-consuming business. It's a process that cannot be rushed and although the materials and designs of contemporary mosaics differ from their ancient predecessors, the stone cutter is the only difference between the way a mosaic is conceived and made in the twenty-first century and how it was done 2,500 years ago.

Helen is attracted to using natural stones which have a relatively limited colour range but an extraordinary variety and depth.

> 'I was mesmerised by the painstaking intricacy of the designs as well as the beauty of the materials and resolved to immerse myself in this ancient artistic practice.'

The beauty of the stones is one of the pleasures of mosaic making but Helen also uses specialised unglazed Winckelmans ceramic tiles and sometimes vitreous glass.

Recent work has included an exciting commission for a mosaic floor panel for the entrance hall of a London house, which is based on an ancient design of an olive wreath with the Greek words for health, life and happiness. A current commission is a wedding mosaic which will reflect the couples' love of books. In between there's experimentation with new techniques, exploring the use of Scottish stone and other local materials, and working on a series inspired by handwriting – which has a close affinity with mosaics.

All stages of the process are immensely enjoyable for Helen, but the actual making of the mosaic gives the greatest pleasure and satisfaction. It is a very immersive and meditative activity. 'I find myself completely absorbed in it and I delight in watching the mosaic slowly evolve and reach completion.'

This work all takes place in a shared studio space in central Edinburgh run by local arts organisation, Out of the Blue. This space works perfectly for Helen, having tried a couple of other workshops when she first arrived in Edinburgh and found they were not quite right. Helen's own area is directly underneath the former classroom's tall sash windows, with bright light flooding in to the workspace and looking out onto the trees of London Road Gardens. It's a compact space with a wide desk and shelves full of intriguing materials, from lozenges of Italian smalti and shells from local beaches, to jars full of hand-cut stones and supplies of specialist ceramic and glass tiles.

She shares the workspace with a graphic novel writer, a screen printer and an illustrator and, rather than being distracting, finds the collegiate atmosphere of hard work and industry very productive. 'It's encouraging being around people who are making and creating and very passionate about what they do.'

Helen is endlessly inspired by classical mosaics – struck by how little understood they are, perceived as formulaic and clumsy, when in fact they are full of artistry, sensitivity and often startling social commentary. She started writing a blog about the history, techniques and philosophy of mosaics in 2013 and this has slowly built up a considerable following. It also allows her to interact with and learn from other mosaic artists around the world.

Since returning from Greece and establishing her practice in Edinburgh, Helen's started to use local stone materials rather than the ones she brought back with her and is full of new ideas and experimentation away from the traditions that she's been taught in. She enjoys walking at Gullane and Tyninghame and picking up shells which

'It's encouraging being around people who are making and creating and very passionate about what they do.'

can be embedded into mosaics, and also visiting the Museum of Scotland to look at the early Celtic stone carvings which are not dissimilar in style to Byzantine designs. Scottish embroidered samplers made by girls and young women are another source of inspiration – they have a lot in common with mosaics in terms of the slow, solitary and precise way in which they are made.

However, her real inspiration comes from looking around. 'The dry-stone dykes which ripple across the countryside, the cobbled streets of the New Town and even configurations of picnickers in public spaces on sunny days are really all just mosaics.' The great thing about mosaics is that inspiration is everywhere. You can get inspired by the pre-existing mid-nineteenth/early twentieth-century mosaic shop thresholds which turn up all over Edinburgh, as well as the more elaborate floor mosaics which were made for public spaces during the same period. For instance, the Virgin office in the main forecourt of Waverley Station has an amazing mosaic that was originally designed when the space was the dining hall of the train workers.

Helen is currently working on a project for a walled garden in Dumfriesshire – the mosaic will go over an archway leading from the main garden into an orchard behind it. Winckelmans tiles will be used because they are extremely durable, frost-proof, and have a greater colour range than stone. The client has given Helen a list of the fruit and vegetables grown in the garden as well as images of a very handsome cockerel living in the orchard, so the design will include these elements from the garden with the cockerel in pride of place striding purposefully over the arch.

Her work as editor of Andamento, the British Association for Modern Mosaics' (BAMM) journal, allows Helen the opportunity to get deeply involved in modern and contemporary mosaic practice beyond her own studio and she helped compile a guide to the mosaics of Scotland to coincide with BAMM's 2017 forum in Edinburgh, which was the first of its kind and provided an insight into the extensive world of mosaics in a Scottish context.

www.helenmilesmosaics.org
www.facebook.com/helenmilesmosaics
Instagram: @helenmilesmosaics
Twitter: @hmmosaics

Namon Gaston

FURNITURE MAKER AND DESIGNER

It was a youthful interest in making and building that eventually led to a love of craftsmanship and design that allows Namon Gaston to produce a diverse range of furniture, designing for commercial production alongside the bespoke manufacture of private commissions.

It all happens in his studio on the outskirts of Edinburgh, adapted from an old mining bath-house building, separated into sections and shared with other timber-based businesses. It's a large, bright space with stacks of wood arranged around the walls and different kinds of heavy machinery spread throughout the workshop. There's a wood-burning stove and, of course, a constant source of fuel!

Initially starting work as a metalworker, it was the creation of a Mackintosh-inspired chair made from wood and metal that uncovered a flair and passion for making furniture. After deciding to take a year's foundation course, Namon went on to Edinburgh College of Art and studied Furniture Design. 'I just fell in love with mid-century design as a whole, not just the furniture, but all aspects of it. It was such an exciting time for design.'

Much of his time studying was spent in the college library hoovering up as much information as he could. He learned about Danish designers going right back to Kaare Klint, who set the movement off in the early 1900s. It was the combination of repeatability of what they produced, combined with such a beautiful aesthetic and a deep respect for the materials used, that inspired him and was a real game changer. When he completed his studies, he found an apprenticeship

with a cabinetmaker in rural Scotland and then, ready to branch out on his own, he set up his own company in Edinburgh in 2005.

Inspired by designers like Borge Mogensen and his utilitarian and simplistic approach, Namon initially created speculative pieces, experimenting with his own style and approach to design. An early commission for a set of dining table and chairs gave him valuable experience, happy clients and a showpiece to secure future work, all the while honing his craft and learning all the skills he needed to work with wood. He appreciates the warmth and textures of the grain and the individuality of the timber; it's a much softer and more tactile material than the metal he started out with. Namon works with all the hand tools any cabinetmaker would have but he also loves using precision machinery. He's found his own way of designing with fine tolerances as well as incorporating traditional craftsmanship into his designs.

Namon's commissions come from a mix of corporate and private clients and whether it's a free-standing work desk or a dining room table and chairs, it's always important to see the client's environment because it will have an influence on how his work will sit in the space.

He knows it's good to see what they already have and get a sense of who the people are – that's all part of the commission process, figuring out who the client is and how he can create and design especially for them. 'I begin with rough sketching on paper; proceed to drafting and then modelling on CAD. This not only allows me to reference drawings and models for production details but also allows me to store all of my designs in a form that would be useful should any of them be reproduced in the future.'

A recent commission has been a boardroom table and twenty-four chairs for the University of Edinburgh. The table is extendable and has been quite the feat to engineer. The chairs are stackable and lightweight for ease of use and all made from beautiful oak. Other recent commissions include a boardroom table for the Dean Gallery in Edinburgh, and furniture for

private clients, Izat Arundell in Porteous' Studio, a luxury apartment created from a disused garage in the centre of Edinburgh. They commissioned all of the interior woodwork including the kitchen cabinetry and the furniture from Namon – created from a single oak tree which was an element that really excited the clients. 'The tree was HUGE and it felt like the *Titanic* coming in when it was delivered!' Using wood from the same tree meant that there was uniformity to the wood throughout the apartment, linking the kitchen with the dining and seating areas.

Generally, Namon sources his wood from a supplier in Glasgow. The company is used to his exacting standards and allows him to come through and sift his way through the materials until he selects the specific boards that will work for his current commissions. All the timber Namon uses is Forest Stewardship Council (FSC) and Programme for the Endorsement of Forest Certification (PEFC) certified.

However, all commissions are different and a recent very special one was to design and produce a Scottish whisky cabinet to house the client's collection of vintage single malts, all created with native timbers. Sourcing the wood took Namon up to Forres in the north where he sourced walnut, and to the West Coast for a particular oak. The sycamore and marble that completed the rare and beautiful palate were also sourced from specific areas of Scotland. 'I am always inspired by function, making something work well and to be beautiful is a constant push for my work.'

The introductory process with clients is very satisfying and being a designer at heart, these initial discussions get the creative juices flowing, relishing how he can bring his own ideas to create what's needed. The Namon Gaston style is simplicity and full of purpose and functionality. If there is a decorative element it will come organically through the production techniques he uses and he always makes sure that every component has a utilitarian reason behind it.

Besides commissioned work, Namon has also designed his own furniture collection that can be made to order with optional bespoke facets should the client want it. He creates a lot of his own tooling, to give consistency and precision in production, ensuring all the designs are repeatable. He enjoys this small-scale craft production, working mostly on precision machinery rather than with the smaller hand tools.

As an alternative to steam bending, any curved components that he produces are made from strips of laminated timber. The strips are all cut from the same board to give consistency, and then laid back together in a mould to produce the form.

'I'm as much a designer as a crafts person, so I can adapt to different processes and materials quite readily. You can get a little stir-crazy working on your own all the time.'

Collaboration is also part of his work and Namon likes to work with different designers on various projects. 'I'm as much a designer as a crafts person, so I can adapt to different processes and materials quite readily. You can get a little stir-crazy working on your own all the time.' There have been partnerships with jewellers, graphic designers and, of course, upholsterers. Peter Holmes from Be Seated recently worked with Namon to create two lounge chairs for a show curated by Design Exhibition Scotland. They also worked together on a mid-century inspired daybed for design studio Instrmnt's flagship store in Glasgow.

Working with private clients is extremely rewarding for Namon, knowing that the pieces he produces for them will become heirlooms and hopefully be handed down through generations. Delivery is a particularly wonderful part of the process, but can be nerve-wracking at the same time. Feedback often comes in the form of an email a couple of days later, when the clients let Namon know how happy they are with his work and how it will be something treasured for the future.

'I think I would say that I am most proud of the type of work that I produce. It has taken a long time and a lot of hard work to build my business to what it is today. All of the experiences along the way have allowed me to hone my particular skillset and I am proud and grateful to be able to do what I love.'

Namon likes to work quietly with humility, working carefully and slowly and hoping that his reputation precedes him. His expert designs and craft come through years of experience, commitment and passion.

In his downtime Namon enjoys a walk up Arthur's Seat with his partner and dog – it's a sure way to appreciate Edinburgh and blow the cobwebs away. He also likes to browse hidden gem antique stores where he might find the odd classic mid-century chair and more inspiration for his own designs.

Namon's award-winning furniture has become synonymous with its high quality, honest design and rich understanding for the materials with which he works. His carefully proportioned and considered furniture has a strong sense of style and integrity. Elegance and subtle detailing prevail, and his pieces are destined to become heirlooms of the future.

www.namongaston.com

www.facebook.com/namongaston
Instagram: @namongaston
Twitter: @namongaston

Lara Scobie

CERAMIC ARTIST

For Lara Scobie, passion for her discipline began at school where she found a lifelong love for creating ceramics. Once she had been introduced to pottery by an inspiring teacher, Lara spent as much time as she could in the class, filling her after-school hours and learning as much of the process as she could. A degree course at Camberwell College of Arts and Crafts in London, where she graduated with honours in Ceramics, was followed by a postgraduate diploma undertaken at Edinburgh College of Art.

Lucky enough to find a tiny studio space in the Adam Pottery in Edinburgh, Lara worked in the shop and the pottery while she began her artistic career and she still has her workshop there today, only in a much larger space! In 1992 Lara was the Premier Award winner of the New Zealand Fletcher Challenge Ceramic Award. Visiting New Zealand to collect the award, she was also invited to tour the country and demonstrate her techniques at different colleges. The following year Lara was a participant in a prestigious Porcelain Workshop in Prague where she met and worked alongside some of Europe's leading porcelain ceramists, later touring the US with them. Winning such a fantastic international award and working with leading international ceramic artists so early in her career brought her work to the attention of the press and a much wider audience, and also brought an invitation to lecture at Duncan of Jordanstone College of Art and Design. Before she knew it, Lara had a job which still allowed her to create and establish herself in her own practice. She now works exclusively as a ceramic artist but this opportunity in academia helped establish her career and allowed her creative freedom.

From the basement studio in Edinburgh's wonderful New Town, Lara works using the process of casting where slip (liquid clay) is poured into plaster moulds to produce forms that are then decorated with a combination of marks including incised drawing (engraving a design by cutting or scraping the clay) into the soft surface and sgraffito (a form of decoration made by scratching a surface to reveal a lower layer of a contrasting colour) through coloured underglaze.

'For me it is the balance between composition and form, absence and presence that offers some of the most exciting opportunities for expressing my creative voice.'

All her work is hand-built in stoneware and bone china clay and decorated with coloured porcelain slip. The surfaces are finished by diamond polishing – a polishing method using hand polishing pads encrusted with flex of tiny diamonds. This is a time-consuming part of the process but nevertheless important as it gives the finished surface a beautiful satin finish.

The plaster moulds that are manufactured to the artist's own specifications create vessels: vases and bowls that can have function but are wonderful statement sculptural pieces and, like a painting on a wall, can sit proudly on a shelf or table, admired for their artistry and the skill of the creator. The forms are purposefully simple: cylindrical and conical asymmetrical shapes that ultimately create a more complex surface. There are large leaning cylinders, vertiginous narrow jugs, elegant beakers and tactile bowls. The shapes have changed and developed over time – widening the cones and cylinders, undulating the top edges – the smallest change in shape can lend a dynamic influence to the finished work. They are all intriguingly off-set, which steers the eye to the beauty of the form and how that sits with the really compelling decoration that draws the viewer in to the deceptively uncomplicated patterns and bold colour choices.

Lara's pattern creation is intuitive. She doesn't work from a sketchbook and prefers getting straight into the organic process of decoration. The pattern starts with a line and everything after is in response to that. It's all done by hand, amazingly using no rulers or mapping out beforehand and the patterns lean much more towards the geometric rather than floral, and the pattern always relates and is complimentary to the form. Initially working in white with black decoration, fabulous strong colour including orange, reds, and yellows have been added to the collections, as well as stunning gold leaf interiors.

For Lara, the theme of balance is a constant, significantly underlining her work in which ideas develop between the lively interplay of form and surface. By integrating drawing, surface mark making and volume, the balance of space and pattern is played with alongside hue and texture on both the decorated and void surface areas. 'For me it is the balance between composition and form, absence and presence that offers some of the most exciting opportunities for expressing my creative voice.'

The most enjoyable part of the process is about mid-way, when the clay is still leather hard and a rhythm has been accomplished in the decorating. The design has been committed to but there are still opportunities to change direction if required. The clay at this stage is particularly fragile and must be handled with great care. Loss of concentration or one careless move could end in disaster.

Because of the process used in ceramics, different pieces are usually being worked on at the same time. Drawing and decoration might be taking place while other pieces are drying off. It's also a time of great anticipation: when the work eventually goes into the kiln, the doors are closed for firing and it is only when the doors are opened after many hours that the true results from the delicate and time-consuming process is revealed.

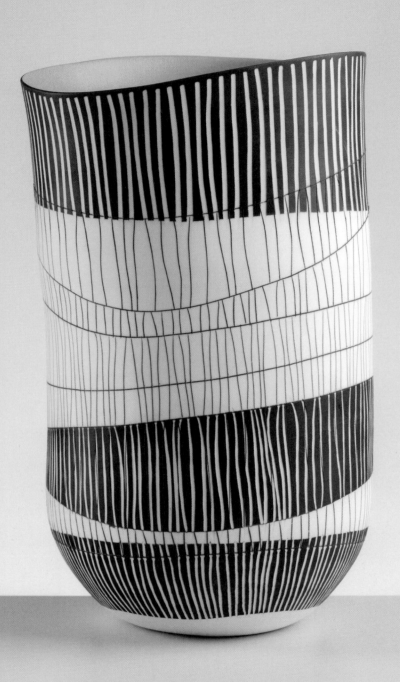

'From the moment a fresh bag of clay is opened my imagination is triggered by the sensory pleasure of its smooth texture and the anticipatory thrill of potential. Working with clay is as exciting and terrifying as a roller coaster ride, presenting as many challenges as rewards.' And the finished pieces are spectacular – the fresh abstract patterns a wonderful contrast against the unglazed high-fired white Parian clay, with interiors popping with intense bright colours – lime green, tangerine and royal blue.

To understand this soft malleable material — really just a lump of wet earth — takes time, but with considered handling and measured judgement it can be manipulated into exciting and expressive form. This transformation goes through many stages as the clay is first shaped, then hardened and dried, before being finally altered by the alchemy of firing to a new ceramic form — hard, durable and permanent.

It's during the most fragile and absorbing part of the process that Lara also finds the most inspiration. 'When I'm in the zone, my hands seem instinctively to know what to do and my mind seems open to new ideas. This is the time when ideas come to me and I have my most creative thinking.' And it is incredible to think that this is also the point when the unplanned, undrawn-out decoration is taking place. Not a process for the faint-hearted but a testament to the skill and experience of the artist that these two creative processes can happen at the same time.

Lara finds that technical expertise and experience are always challenged by each different set of influences, from pragmatic considerations to artistic instinct. It's this space between that she is most interested in – where technique, material and creative insight meet. This 'space between' can also be found in negative shapes in the countryside where Lara goes to escape the city and allow the ideas formed during her process to consolidate in her mind. The shapes of spaces between fence posts, between trees in a forest, the vertical lines and planes beside one another inspire the mark making and flow of the decoration she uses. The rolling of the hilly landscape around Edinburgh or in the centre at Arthur's Seat can be seen exquisitely recreated in her most recent pieces.

Currently working towards a solo exhibition at The Scottish Gallery in Edinburgh supported by Creative Scotland, Lara has recently been awarded an artist's development grant. This grant brings the joy of freedom of experimentation, working with new colours and materials, and bringing new ideas to the collection that will be on display in 2019. She finds this opportunity both scary and thrilling at the same time and it's a wonderful platform to create a cohesive display that represents her work in different sizes and a balance in colour and pattern.

Besides the Adam Pottery in Edinburgh, other opportunities to see Lara's work are at specialist ceramic fairs, bringing her work to the attention of collectors and clients that understand and respect the medium she works in. Her work can be found in public and private collections in museums throughout the UK, US and Europe.

www.larascobie-ceramics.com

www.facebook.com/LaraScobieCeramics
Instagram: @larascobie

Misun Won

JEWELLERY DESIGNER/MAKER

Misun Won began her career as a jeweller by studying for a BA in Fine Art and Precious Metal Design at Hanyang University in South Korea and completed her education with a Masters in Jewellery and Silversmithing at Edinburgh College of Art. 'My extensive experience of living and working in both Britain and South Korea has given me the broader cultural outlook I sought when moving away from home. It has enabled me to position myself in what I call 'neutral territory' and to examine both cultures with fresh eyes.'

From a very young age Misun was interested in making things by hand, particularly enjoying the different textures in working with paper, clay and cloth. Fashion magazines were collected and poured over, informing her understanding of how jewellery communicates with cloth, and with the human body. Going to university to study jewellery-making was then a natural progression that also gave her an understanding of how jewellery has played a significant role in subtly conveying the society and beauty of Korean women.

'The influences of both countries can be seen in my work: a major inspiration is Korean patchwork, but this highly traditional form is interpreted by me through Western fractal geometry.'

After studying as an undergraduate in South Korea, Misun wanted to explore new cultures over a more extended period of time in order to develop a new approach to her creative practice. She wanted to come to the UK after seeing Dorothy Hogg's work online. 'I was immediately hooked on her jewellery. I particularly liked the way she interpreted the human organ and its relationship with the body. I was also very impressed by the beauty of the materials she chose.' Dorothy Hogg is an internationally recognised jeweller and was head of Edinburgh College of Art's Jewellery and Silversmithing department for almost twenty years. After a long-distance telephone conversation, Ms Hogg invited Misun to become part of the course in Edinburgh. 'The influences of both countries can be seen in my work: a major inspiration is Korean patchwork, but this highly traditional form is interpreted by me through Western fractal geometry.' Korean patchwork or 'Jogakbo' was developed as a means of wrapping an object or food in a careful and respectful way. The ancient Korean people believed that keeping something wrapped was tantamount to keeping good fortune. Misun took a course on Boudoir Handicraft, or 'Kubang Gongye' in Korean, that included Jogakbo to further develop her work.

This particular genre of craft has been practiced widely among housewives in Korea since the dynasty of Joseon (1392–1897). As Neo-Confucianism was established as the state ideology, which restricted women's role in society, taking good care of the household was regarded as the most important virtue during this time. However, in contemporary Korean society the craft is still practiced by women today as a celebration of craft heritage from the Joseon dynasty.

Fractals are non-geometric shapes that have the same degree of non-regularity on all scales. These repeat patterns are found all around us in nature and we can see how these two inspirations have informed Misun's delicately organic work. Using a wrapped structure also allows Misun to convey the same meaning of value and good fortune in the pieces she creates. Her in-depth study in the art of fractal geometry and Jogakbo helps her to create these dynamic structures for her collection. She feels as if the meditative making process is an act of prayer for wearers as the act of imbuing auspicious qualities within her jewellery parallels the wish of ancient Korean housewives who made Jogakbo for their family members. In this regard, Misun's jewellery is not only a body ornament but it functions also as a lucky charm for wearers.

Misun has used the circle shape to develop a variety of complex, handmade contemporary jewellery forms in silver and gold, and sometimes with copper and brass. Her wonderful, wearable collections include necklaces, rings, earrings and brooches constructed using rhythmical structures and patterns either on their own or in combination with coloured threads, Korean braiding and silk cord. Many of the individual pieces appear to build up architecturally, creating the appearance of an organic structure. Exquisite earrings and rings can appear like flowers ready to open and brooches reminiscent of garlands – delightful in their simplicity but very complex in their creation. The eye is drawn to how the materials work together, how the individual shapes create the complete form, and one imagines them to be very tactile, reassuring art objects to wear. Along with the silver, oxidized silver, gold and other metals, she includes pearls and precious stones in monochrome tones and occasionally a flash of bright red or blue from the Korean braiding or silk rope. Besides the jewellery collection Misun has also created a range of simple vessels in silver that have her signature circular shapes flowing from the rim or around the base of the cups.

Misun begins her process by drawing out a paper sample in intricate and repetitive shapes. The paper is then cut and folded as a perfect template for the piece of jewellery she is about to create. Making the paper samples is time-consuming and must be accurate so that the form and design can be copied precisely onto the precious metals she works with. The paper structures are themselves works of great beauty and she's often had people ask to buy them from her at Open Studio events. But they are too valuable and meaningful to her to sell. Creating the paper samples by hand rather than using digital technology helps Misun visualise the finished work and the time and space needed for doing this part of the process helps inform designs and shapes. Once Misun is satisfied with the structure she gets excited to start creating it in metal.

The techniques she uses to make her collections appear simple but the skills needed for the processes come from many years of practice. 'I use hand-sawing, scraping, burnishing and soldering. These basic techniques allow me to have direct contact with the materials and to understand better the structure of my work.' The working process could be categorized as painstaking and slow, especially the cutting by hand straight from the silver sheets. 'I often get asked if I shouldn't design the patterns and structure with digital technology and then make my work with laser cutters and other machines, but I couldn't – it's almost like a conversation with the material for me.' She presumes it would be much faster but Misun enjoys the touch and feel of all the elements she uses, whether it's silver or gold or copper

> 'I use hand-sawing, scraping, burnishing and soldering. These basic techniques allow me to have direct contact with the materials and to understand better the structure of my work.'

or brass. And having worked and developed these processes over twenty years, her hands are now trained and strong enough for sustained periods of work.

Another technique Misun uses is Keum-boo: thin gold foil is placed on the object and a polished steel burnisher tacks it down and then presses it over the surface, fixing it permanently in place. The gold will not stick until the correct temperature is reached. If a hot plate is used generally a thickish piece of steel, copper or brass is used to transfer the heat more smoothly to the sheet silver being applied with gold foil. It's another painstaking and skilful process that allows the jeweller to press form into the simple but complex, almost architectural, structures.

Misun has her studio space at Coburg House in Leith. It's a small cosy space but with enough room for everything she needs. Patterns and templates adorn the walls, along with images of her stunning and innovative work. Her trusty collection of tools are well worn. Different coloured braiding lies on her worktop, ready to use and there are samples of Korean patchwork visible. Her mood board is covered in cut-outs from fashion magazines – inspirations for future work. She enjoys the confidence of working alone but also appreciates being close to other artists or designer/makers like herself, whatever their discipline. Ideas come from conversations with other artists, as well as information about shows and exhibitions that may be perfect for Misun's work. Other inspiration comes from the variety of exhibitions available in Edinburgh and trips to the National Museum of Scotland – a priority on any artist's itinerary when visiting or living in the city – allows Misun to draw inspiration from the many ancient art objects in display.

Misun has presented her work internationally, most recently at Inhorgenta in Germany, SOFA Chicago and also in New York. Craft Scotland has represented her jewellery at Collect London on various occasions. She regularly exhibits at Goldsmiths in London and also Elements in Edinburgh. For Misun, taking part in these shows with other Scottish makers has been amongst the proudest moments in her career. 'Professionally I think of myself as a jewellery designer/ maker based in Scotland, although it could be argued that I am in fact a Scottish maker.'

Misun is currently developing a new body of work in gold. She'd like to explore the powerful value and colour that the material could convey with a range of newly developed patterns.

www.misunwonjewellery.com

www.facebook.com/misunwonjewellery
Instagram: misunwonjewellery
Twitter: @MW_jewellery

Lucy Engels

TEXTILE DESIGNER AND PRINTMAKER

The first thing you see when you enter Lucy Engels' studio is the fabulous quilt she's created that's hanging on the wall. It's the Test Card Quilt that very recently had pride of place at the Craft Scotland Summer Exhibition and was selected for exhibit at QuiltCon 2018 International Modern Quilt Guild Exhibition. It encapsulates her love of colour and the precision and expertise required to create these functional works of art.

Lucy studied at Gray's School of Art in Aberdeen and gained a BA (Hons) in Fine Art, Printmaking but took a rather alternative route to where she is now. On leaving university she at first wanted to make a living through her prints and other artwork. But the reality of how difficult it can be to get a gallery to represent you when you're just out of art school meant that Lucy had to make some tough decisions. She decided that retraining was the best thing to do and gained a Master of Social Work (MSW) from Edinburgh University and so found herself on an entirely different career path. Fast forward to five years ago and out of the blue Lucy dusted off her sewing machine and decided to make a quilt for her newborn nephew. She revelled in the fact that the process was clean – as opposed to messy when printmaking. It also allowed her to think again about pattern and colour. 'I embraced the process, which I found was unexpectedly similar to printmaking. It has to be exact, layers create the final quilt, texture can be added to create dimension.'

She's so glad she decided to make that quilt as it brought her to where she is now: running a successful business centred on the quilts and her screen printed and block printed designs for fabric that play between traditional hand-drawn motifs and geometric form. Once her nephew's quilt was finished, Lucy found she couldn't stop making them and an obsession with quilts was born. Things snowballed from that point and besides her quilts she also uses the technique to create a range of bags and other home accessories. The printed material that she creates is also popular with customers who like to buy the beautiful designs to use in their own quilting projects.

The origin of traditional quilting methods is believed to have come from ancient Egypt and is widely celebrated in the US. It's a tradition that has not changed much over time, apart from the use of the automated sewing machine! Historians have discovered that quilting and piecing were used for clothing and furnishings in diverse parts of the world from very early times.

Lucy's process is very hands-on, developing her ideas through testing with materials rather than sketching out ideas. She loves variety, often producing one-off pieces and taking commissions for special projects. 'My ideas for quilts happen quite organically. Cutting and moving fabric around on my design wall similar to the actions of a painter. I feel lucky that I am able to produce my products from start to finish and I can also manufacture small batches of my accessories ranges as and when I need to.'

Colour is her main inspiration. Most often she begins with a carefully selected colour palette and develops her ideas from there. She also strives to retain a printmaker quality to her work when creating images for her fabric, hand drawing and screen printing directly on to the fabric that she uses. She also loves the versatility of quilts. 'When I make quilts, I make them with the idea they're going on a wall and it just so happens you can also use it on a bed!' When Lucy makes a quilt, she's also conscious that she's making a piece that will potentially become an heirloom and enjoys the fact that it can be used by every generation in a family.

Testing new patterns and trying new colour combinations is a favourite element of her process but it's something that there never seems to be quite enough time for. There is time, though, for the finishing and hand binding of her quilts and Lucy finds this step satisfying. 'It's a slow process but it gives me a chance to check over my work and spend the last bit of time with the quilt before it goes to its new home. I get very attached to them.'

A sewing machine is used for most of the quilting but Lucy also uses the hand-stitched English paper piecing method when creating textile art. English paper piecing is a method of stabilizing fabric around a heavy paper shape before sewing the pieces together to create intricately pieced designs. It provides excellent accuracy and precision and suits Lucy's method of finding pattern in colour and shape.

Lucy's wonderful new range of bags are also quilted. The materials are gathered together and pieces moved around till Lucy finds the best way to pull the colours and pattern together. The quilting method gives the bag texture and structure, and each one is different so any lucky customer is really getting a completely unique and functional work of art.

The material used for her ranges of delightful screen-printed make-up and toiletry bags, fabric baskets and cushion covers, is created in a very traditional way. Lucy hand-draws the separations for screen printing and completes the process by hand printing. Each collection is limited in number, with fabric designs being printed for only a few months at a time. Make-up bags are produced in numbered editions of 100. The relatively quick turnover of designs and patterns that Lucy creates reflect her high energy and passion for the work she is creating, and also her desire to keep offering her customers something fresh and new.

Creating sustainable and environmentally friendly work is also important and Lucy uses the best natural cotton fabrics and eco-friendly water-based inks that will have been heat set for durability. Every last piece of fabric is used in her process to reduce waste and you can also pop her designs into the washing machine so they can be used again and again.

Lucy's business has found fans and grown through social media where her authentic delight in her work is infectious, and she pulls enthusiastic customers along with her on to the next project. Social media has also allowed Lucy to become part of a worldwide quilting community which provides endless positive support and encouragement; she's very appreciative of that and the many other opportunities and connections that have been made online.

Working in a shared studio space with other talented makers, Lucy's part of the studio has large windows and there is a tumble of wonderful fabrics lying ready to be made into her designs. There's also a pile of gorgeous quilts and the camera is always at hand as Lucy takes all her images herself. The wall holds sheets of pinned paper with splashes of stimulating colour for ideas and tests, and the whole atmosphere is one of industry and texture. The studio complex is based in an old Victorian primary school not far from Edinburgh city centre. There's high ceilings and excellent light. Within the building there is a print studio, as well as wood and ceramics workshops.

'When I make quilts, I make them with the idea they're going on a wall and it just so happens you can also use it on a bed!'

91

Lucy compromises having her own studio space to be able to have access to these other workshops but she does enjoy sharing with other artists whose mutual encouragement and support she finds motivating and has often led to exciting collaborations or working in new directions.

There's an exciting plan ahead to create screen prints that are solely works of art, taking things back to her printmaker roots. A collection of postcard sized prints has already been very successful and there are more of these small works of art to come. Lucy definitely doesn't feel that any of the years between art school and making that quilt for her nephew have been wasted in any way. It would never have produced the same outcome and she is so happy and successful in her business today that there is no time for looking back, only forward. Next year's collection is already being planned and Lucy enjoys visits to Cramond Island to get a clear head space and a bit of distance from the bustle of the city – and it's also a fantastic spot for taking images of her wonderful quilts! Living in Leith has also provided attractive textured backdrops for art projects and the Botanic Gardens at Inverleith is a constant source of inspiration for her hand-drawn motifs.

'I am proud that I am able to make a living from something I enjoy endlessly, that I have created a business that brings people joy and where I have complete control from product development and photography to marketing and finances.'

The next holiday season is coming up soon and preparations are already being made for what will be a very busy time. Concentrating mostly on selling online, Lucy also exhibits at events like Handmade Edinburgh, #Cloth and the Craft Scotland Summer Shows. Lucy's work can also be found in a few select retail outlets throughout the UK.

www.lucyengels.com

Instagram: @_lucyengels
Twitter: @malinkyquilts

Jonathan Pang

FURNITURE DESIGNER/MAKER

There's plenty of daylight streaming into Jonathan Pang's extremely neat and tidy studio. The wall space has been utilised for the storage of fixings and fasteners, and offcuts of materials and tools. He freely admits that he and his studio-mate suffer from workshop OCD and they like to use the hoover frequently! But one can understand this neatness and streamlining when looking at Jonathan's furniture. His passion is for simple, elegant designs incorporating subtle yet intricate detail and he has a fabulous back catalogue of his free-standing furniture designs to show potential clients.

Graduating from the Glasgow College of Building and Printing in 2000 with a diploma in Furniture Construction and Design, Jonathan has worked for some of the leading furniture companies in Scotland. Having gained vast knowledge within the woodworking industry, Jonathan Pang Furniture was established in 2015 with a focus on small-scale batch production pieces that were both tactile and functional. Born with a practical side, Lego played a huge part in his childhood and he also had a little chest of tools that he enjoyed working with – evidence from an early age that creating and building were going to be part of his life in some way.

'Wood has allowed me to shape and form ideas fairly easily and create pieces of furniture that people want to interact with.'

Inspired by the clean lines and aesthetic of mid-century Scandinavian designers, Jonathan is also fascinated by Japanese design. He really appreciates the complex detailing involved and the process of interlocking timber by cutting intricate pieces and fitting them together perfectly without any other element. The Japanese also build large structures, their decorative temples, for example, using the same underlying process – where the building will be supported by interlocking pins that hold the construction together. It's a curious form of construction that has influenced his own work when designing and manufacturing custom pieces of furniture, reflecting Jonathan's enjoyment of blending timbers together with other materials and with a special love of precise and complex joinery.

The first commission, once Jonathan had decided to establish his own business and become self-employed, was the *Walls Desk – Fumed Oak & Brass Writing Desk*. This was a private commission made from European Oak, fumed with ammonia to give its distinct deep tone and highlighted with the use of polished brass runners that connect into the handle area. The desktop incorporates a slightly raised rim around both its sides and back. A joy to make, this first independent work allowed him to impose his own personal style, adding the lip and brass features, fuming the oak. Taking his time over the craftsmanship and the success of the finished work brought new clients to the new business. It also brought an invitation to exhibit at the prestigious London Design Festival in 2017 and so he designed the *Phoem Collection* of a table, lamp and chair. He wanted to create lightweight structures that could be folded down so began the creative process by designing the table and then taking away the excess weight and following the same blueprint for the chair and lamp. The result was a standout collection that was an entirely new style and introduced US companies to his work as well as more commissions closer to home.

For Collect 2018 – the craft sector's premier showcase – an exploration into recyclable materials and his love of Japanese puzzle boxes led to the creation of a patterned box and a glass case made from Richlite – an incredibly durable, extremely versatile and highly sustainable material made from resin-infused paper. Richlite has been around since the 1970s but is becoming more popular now as designers like Jonathan, who also creates his collections from certified and responsible timber sources, care more about sustainability and the environmental impact of their work.

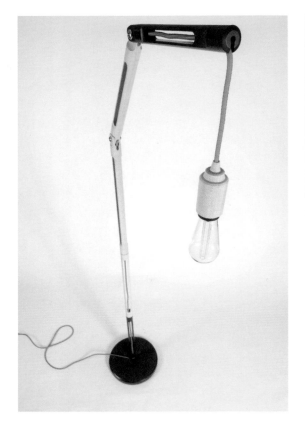

Jonathan's studio space leads off from a central machine workshop that is shared with other cabinetmakers and designers working with wood in the same complex. He is constantly stimulated by colleagues of the same discipline who can understand the techniques and can be there to offer different approaches or discuss a process when needed, and vice versa. The machine room stores all the timber and has an impressive array of CNC (Computer Numerical Control) machinery, and it's this equipment that Jonathan worked with to create the Richlite boxes. Computerised machinery has contributed to many complicated designs being realised at a fraction of the time it would take by hand, and his own workshop also has the luxury of some smaller machines to aid manufacture. 'I utilise CNC machinery wherever I can. This comes into play when there are numerous components that are much more efficiently made by machine than by hand. In saying that, there will always be traditional methods within my work process. It's a balance between productivity, accuracy and time.'

The bulk of Jonathan's business comes from private commissions, and this process begins with a client meeting to discuss their ideas, what they would like and to see where an idea can go. If the client knows exactly what they want and how it will look, manufacture will begin from a set of working drawings. If the brief is open, then some conceptual drawings are generated with various ideas. Once a drawing is finalised, Jonathan will then take this to the manufacturing side and begin selecting timber or other materials. Jonathan no longer sketches but starts straight away in CAD and it's easy to take a shape and develop from there. It's perfect for helping clients to visualise what the finished piece of furniture will be like. With CAD, elements can be added in or removed easily so it's a time-saving aid for designer and client alike.

For Jonathan, wood has always been the best material to work with and, twenty-one years from when he started, he is still in love with it. 'Wood has allowed me to shape and form ideas fairly easily and create pieces of furniture that people want to interact with.'

He's a big fan of maple, finding it clean and flawless, easy to shape and holding a beautiful finish. Norwegian birch ply is another favourite, along with oak. Preferring lighter woods to dark is more in keeping with the Scandinavian and Japanese aesthetic Jonathan prefers. Clients like to come to the workshop to see the different woods and enjoy being in the studio space with the designer – and he also enjoys visiting the client and seeing where the work will sit; how it will interact with the space it's going to live in and fit with the general lifestyle of the client's habitat. It's mostly domestic clients that commission something special; it's a luxury for them and a pleasure for Jonathan, creating something that will ultimately become a family heirloom.

New technologies and techniques are ever advancing the way timber designs are being built and joined and this furniture maker finds this aspect incredibly exciting. There is so much still to be manufactured in timber and Jonathan enjoys taking photos, collecting images, collating an archive of details that can influence new work. He's constantly thinking about new designs and is enthusiastic from the initial client discussion stage right through to the manufacturing, always fully engaged in each part of the process, and loving every minute.

Relaxation is a family stroll through the National Museum of Scotland, where exciting fresh directions can always be found. Cultural trips to art galleries during family holidays to Berlin and Barcelona are also perfect for replenishing the creative soul.

For the future Jonathan will still prefer to make bespoke free-standing pieces and thoroughly enjoys taking a finished piece of furniture to the client's home or office and setting it in place. It's always a proud moment, and ranks up there beside establishing his own successful business.

A recent recipient of a prestigious Inches Carr Trust Award to produce new work with sustainable materials and incorporating them within the furniture industry, Jonathan can spend some time deciding what compositions will come from it. No doubt it will involve his speciality of blending timber and sheet metal in some way and intricate and beautifully produced joinery elements. It's the combination of all the finishing details that he enjoys adding to his designs that give his work a recognisable signature. Current work includes kitchen furniture and a set of table and chairs for a private client. There's also a set of complicated walnut stools in the pipeline. It can be daunting setting up your own business but, for Jonathan, it has obviously been the right decision. Having received such recognition from the industry through exhibitions and awards, the business will no doubt go from strength to strength.

www.jonathanpangfurniture.com
www.facebook.com/pg/jonathanpangfurniture
Instagram: @jonathanpangfurniture

Myer Halliday

DESIGNER/MAKER

In 2009, Myer graduated from the pioneering part-time Ceramics degree course at the Glasgow School of Art (GSA). He's not sure exactly when his love for the discipline began – it could have been a weekend course he did as a teenager, or later when at secondary school he decided he'd had enough of Russian and persuaded the art department to let him come and mess up their staffroom – which also housed the pottery department. Or when he managed to get an O' Level in the craft. Whenever it was, things have come full circle as he's now running a successful business from Midlothian Innovation Centre in Roslin, just outside Edinburgh.

For many years, playing with clay was one of a number of creative things Myer did in his non-work time. He first worked in education and then moved into social work as part of a support network for students working in a hospital. He thoroughly enjoyed this part of his career – and being part of a team who all worked together to get the job done.

Then Archie McColl, a successful working ceramicist originally from Dumfries, and Head of Department at GSA, introduced the innovative part-time BA (Hons) degree programme which is delivered through residential schools and online distance learning. 'I'd known Archie since I was a child and I was fortunate to get a place on that first year of the course and graduated in 2009. This was a wonderful opportunity for those of us with work and families who couldn't afford to give it up to study for a full-time degree.'

Myer spent many years practicing as a studio potter, however, he was introduced to slip casting while at GSA. This is a way of making ceramic work with plaster moulds and liquid clay, called slip. As someone who has always been interested in the whole range of functional ceramic making – studio work and more commercial factory-made ware – he found this fascinating. Later on, he was introduced to Parian ware (Parian is a particular form of porcelain) that works best in slip form and then Myer embraced slip casting wholeheartedly.

Now Myer creates collections that include functional vases, vessels, plates and bowls. For each design he carefully considers three key themes: pattern, presentation and mark-making.

Pattern, specifically the way in which two-dimensional surface decoration alters your perception of three-dimensional forms, transforms Myer's simple shapes into functional statement pieces that fit into your lifestyle. He particularly enjoys exploring the tension in pattern: his linear, graphic style investigates the spaces between our human desire for predictability and the joy associated with novelty.

Myer's delicate yet durable work explores the visual relationship in the presentation of objects and their environment. While his surface pattern alters our perception, the shape of each object is carefully considered as a series, so his pieces form a cohesive, easy-to-use collection of purposeful objects that fit into any space.

Each piece demonstrates an ongoing love of abstract mark-making and quality of line. His bold, graphic marks interact in beautiful contrast with Myer's materials: namely paper-like porcelaneous clays, creating a simplistic, infinitely usable object designed for everyday life. He takes particular pleasure in making a familiar object slightly unfamiliar, designed in a certain offset way so that there's a question about it.

'For a while now I've been interested in the ways in which, through accumulation or accretion, individual lines or marks add together to create a repetitive pattern which is greater than the sum of the individual lines. Lines are drawn in parallel or crossed or laid over each other, often in a mechanistic, predetermined manner. The way in which the incidental marks (for example, throwing rings) made in the process of making the piece, interact with the drawn pattern is also of interest and adds a further dimension to the decoration.'

Myer feels himself very fortunate to have a workspace that fits exactly what he needs to make his work. He now has a full-time staff member and there's room for expansion if needs be. It's a large, multi-use workspace which allows room for all the back office administration work – dealing with orders and getting them out. There's excellent storage space (moulds take up a lot of room!), a kiln area and decent size workshop where hundreds of pieces can

'I've been interested in the ways in which, through accumulation or accretion, individual lines or marks add together to create a repetitive pattern which is greater than the sum of the individual lines.'

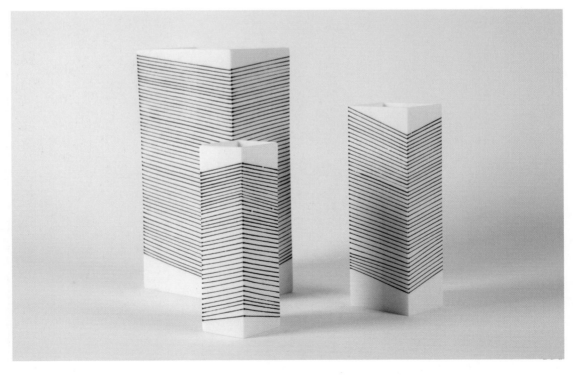

be made each week. Perhaps the best bit though is that the building complex houses a collection of businesses ranging from wave technology companies to high-end craft and design businesses. 'It's wonderful to be part of that type of creative community. Even better is that it's set at the foot of the Pentland Hills which we try and take advantage of when the sun is shining!'

Myer has always had a love of design, an almost unconscious absorbing of shapes, forms and angles as well as illustrations from children's books that still inform his work today. His mother ran a gift shop in the Borders with beautiful Scandinavian design in the range. He thinks this may have given him an eye for what might sell, for what people like to see – and it's also meant that the business side feels quite natural. It's why he likes the term designer/maker to describe himself: 'I'm happy with "maker" because this reflects how I spend the largest proportion of most working days – which is hands-on hands-in clay (and plaster) … but I also think of myself as a designer, working out what and how to make and not necessarily tied to one material, and this is how I would like to be spending more of my time. I also think of myself as a businessman because, fundamentally, I need to fund myself – and the people who work with me – and my

making, and that occupies a lot of my time – trying to make the business work and grow in a sustainable way.'

Recent work has included marbling, which sits beautifully with the range of greys, blacks and ivories. Candle holders, jugs and fruit bowls have been added to the collection. The decoration ranges from graphic lines, dots and circles to no decoration at all. 'The processes I use have been used for hundreds of years. I think that if someone from the 1700s came to where we work they would probably feel quite at home. Although certain peripheral things have changed the tools and techniques we use are the same.'

Last year he began supplying Heal's department store in London with a range of his products and was inspired by the business relationship he enjoyed with them, working as a team to develop his signature style across other ranges. Elements of his designs were used to create textiles for chairs, lampshades and tableware. 'While on a promotional visit to Heal's, I got my photograph taken next to a lampshade with my drawing and I got such a kick out of that!'

The fact that small batch production is possible within his own studio is something that excites Myer, allowing him to see what's possible and how the business could grow and how art can be made more accessible to all. He really appreciates working in collaboration with other designers and craftspeople and has exhibited collaborative work at the London Design Festival with Craft Scotland. With upholsterer Eve Hynd, he exhibited a leather chair, a porcelain gold-leaf stool and a small table.

Besides continuing to supply Heal's, the Myer Halliday brand has also been really fortunate in forging a new relationship with a customer in Japan. The Francfranc Corporation is establishing a world craft centre in Kyoto and they have asked Myer to produce a collection for that – quite an honour! There are stockists throughout the UK including the V&A Dundee, the Design Museum in Kensington, and The Biscuit Factory in Newcastle. This year will also see the first international trade fairs where Myer will be exhibiting with Craft Scotland at NY Now in New York and later at Maison Objet in Paris.

Myer feels really grateful to be part of the industry he's making his way in and, in his own way, having a degree of success in it. 'There are other things that matter too – when a piece first comes out of the mould all fresh and new, in a wee way it's like a birth. It's the same when a completed piece comes out of the mould – some pieces are just right and those ones sing and that is quite wonderful.'

www.myerhalliday.co.uk
Instagram: @myerhalliday

Veronica Rose

KILTMAKER

Former dancer Veronica Rose combines her knowledge of body movement and her expert sewing skills to create perfect kilts in a variety of materials for a diverse and delighted clientele.

Training in Theatre Arts at the Italia Conti Stage School in London was when Veronica's love of fashion and the arts really manifested itself. As a child, her two main interests were dancing and sewing and these skills came together when she was offered an apprenticeship as a kiltmaker out of the blue while back home on holiday in Edinburgh. Working for a busy company on the Royal Mile, she learned all aspects of tailoring and kiltmaking.

A kilt is basically a pleated, wrapped skirt, mostly worn by men, in a tartan of medium or heavy weight wool cloth. The pleats are formed on the back half, and the front half (the apron) is made with two overlapping panels. The craftsmanship comes from the ability to work with a continuous length of 8 yards (the average kilt length), and create a precisely pleated kilt that sits beautifully while worn and will swing with energy and gusto while dancing and walking, with the pleats falling back into perfect position again when standing still. Traditionally handmade, the hand-stitching is important as it takes the pressure out of the stitch, leaving the fabric strong. Considering a kilt is meant to last a lifetime, it needs to withstand years of wear and tear.

After a two-year apprenticeship, Veronica started up on her own under the brand name Rosekilts. With an investment of £20, a Singer treadle sewing machine, a pair of scissors and an iron, she was ready to go. Initially out-working for other companies, she began to build her own clientele, offering traditional and contemporary kilts.

With a traditional kilt, the working process may start with a discussion with the client about family heritage and what tartans might be available and suitable. Sometimes this can involve a lot of research to find the right tartan and then the cloth itself may have to be handwoven especially if it's not in stock at any of the Scottish weaving mills. Veronica also enjoys designing bespoke tartans and working closely with the mill to achieve the exact yarn colour requirements. Contemporary kilt making can be very different and Veronica can work with all kinds of fabrics including synthetics, leather and denim. On a traditional kilt, the selvedge edge is always used and a hem isn't necessary – the weight of the cloth could be too bulky anyway, but with lighter weight materials, like synthetics and some denims, hemming is fine but it's an extra element that needs to work with the movement and precision of the pleats and needs just as much skill. 'I like to work closely with the client to get their vision so they can have as much or as little input as they wish. My clients inspire me completely. My job is to make them feel confident and look fantastic.'

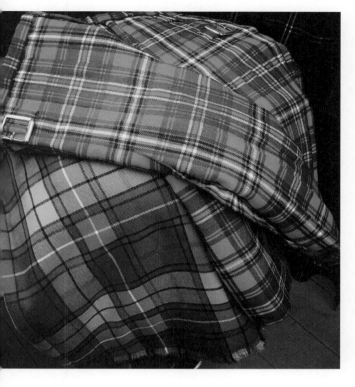

As a former dancer, Veronica has a good insight into how the body moves which is especially useful for making, altering and repairing kilts. Once the material is decided upon, all the measurements are taken and Veronica's expertise can tell how a young person's body will grow, so she'll be able to advise about how the kilt should be made now so that it can be altered easily as time goes on.

With her trusty tools of leather punches, scissors, heavy duty press, pincushion and the tailor's thimble she can't do without, Veronica can get on with creating the kilt. She prefers a method of organised chaos – working on a few kilts at a time, rather than just one. The old treadle machine is used for little finishing touches, but everything else is done by hand and having made hundreds of kilts over the previous twenty-five years she can complete one in six hours. This ability to work fast without loss of craftsmanship is just what's needed to service the many tourists who might be passing through the city on a short holiday, but still want to take a beautiful handmade kilt home with them.

Her clients love coming to her studio at Coburg House in Leith – whether it's by appointment or during the Open Studio weekends. With bolts of fabulous cloths lying around and kilts at different stages of completion, the studio is always a whirl of colour. It's also crammed with haberdashery, leather, threads and other materials, managing to appear cluttered and efficient at the same time. There are prints on the walls that give an idea of the history of the kilt – generally thought to originate at the end of the sixteenth century. It first appeared as a belted plaid or 'great kilt/Feileadh Mhor' which was a full-length garment whose upper half could be used as a cloak draped over the shoulder or brought over the head as a hood. The 'small kilt', similar to the modern-day kilt, did not really develop until the end of the seventeenth and beginning of the eighteenth century, and is essentially the bottom half of the great kilt. Of course, the kilt or belted plaid is also intrinsically wrapped up in Scottish history, having been outlawed in 1746 after the Jacobite Rebellion. This law was repealed in 1782 and happily now kilts can be worn by anyone anywhere!

The wide array of people including singers, dancers and pipers that she comes across on a daily basis is endless. 'It's most enjoyable meeting people from all over the world. I love that my kilts travel internationally and have a whole life of their own after leaving my studio.' There's a lifelong connection to the kilt as it can be handed down or passed across the generations. Rosekilts also

specialises in the restoration of vintage kilts and jackets, and has been known to recycle wools and turn them into something completely different. Sustainability is something the kiltmaker is very passionate about, and Veronica loves the fact that the garments can be passed on, altered, re-worked and recycled in different ways, testament to the strength of the cloth and the beauty of the workmanship. The business is very seasonal: springtime is wedding season; summer belongs to the graduates and tourists; autumn brings back-to-school kilts and the invisible mending of damaged kilts, while winter is the season for ceilidhs, parties and every kind of celebration you can think of. 'My loyal clients keep coming back and recommending me. They push me to keep motivated and continue reinventing a classic.'

Corporate clients can also bring a completely fresh and exciting order. For example, Rosekilts has been commissioned by restaurateur, Marco Pierre White, to create bespoke tweed kilts, leather-edged waistcoats and sporrans for the staff in his new restaurant in Singapore. Another recent order was from the whisky brand Johnny Walker to create thirty kilts for their area managers.

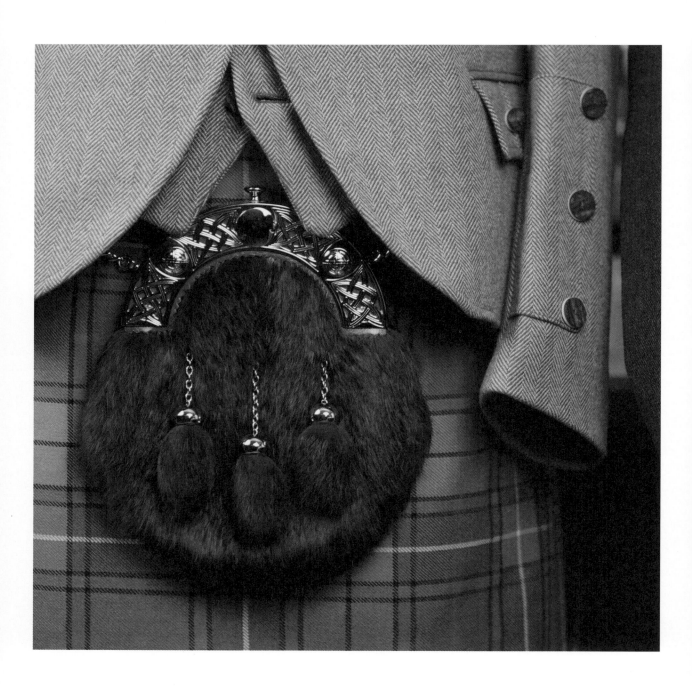

'Kilts and dancing are so inextricably linked. It's wonderful how my two passions have interwoven in a way I could never have foreseen when I first embarked on this beautiful journey.'

It's just as well Veronica enjoys the solitude of working in her studio, listening to music, thinking creatively about new ideas and projects while sewing away, with so many commissions to do. The time is precious, with family responsibilities to deal with as well as running a successful business.

Rosekilts' success has come from word of mouth and now there's a growing following on Instagram. It's truly international with recent clients from as far away as Mexico and Asia. 'It's so easy to snap studio pictures of fresh pieces and instantly upload these. I get to share with my fellow makers from around the world the wonderful colours and textures which bring so much warmth into a glossy arena and something a little different, I think.'

Besides the day-to-day kiltmaking, there are often commissions from film companies to create costumes for productions. Veronica also designs and creates her own range of leather sporrans. The perfect accessory to the kilt, of course, they can be created bespoke or are available in a ready-to-wear collection.

With the world flooding into Edinburgh every August, Veronica finds the buzz of it inspiring but once it's over, she likes to leave the city and travel north to Stonehaven for a break away from it all, coming back regenerated and ready for the next season of kilts.

'Kilts and dancing are so inextricably linked. It's wonderful how my two passions have interwoven in a way I could never have foreseen when I first embarked on this beautiful journey.'

www.rosekilts.com

www.facebook.com/rosekilts
Instagram: @kiltqueen
Twitter: @kiltqueen

Bryony Knox

SILVERSMITH

Bryony's elegant work brings a hint of humour and glamour to the simple items we use in our daily rituals. From the theatrical to the everyday, the designs cleverly combine figurative sculpture and functionality with a large dollop of wit. Her work is based on a love of storytelling, movement and colour. Creatures and characters are brought to life in sculptural silverware through the traditional techniques of chasing and repoussé.

Inspiration comes from an interest in the illustrated stories, myths and nursery rhymes of her childhood; from her first Ladybird book of Greek myths to the German cautionary tale of *Struwwelpeter*; from Sing A Song of Sixpence to Edward Lear's nonsense poems. Hundreds of years ago her family was Huguenot silversmiths so maybe a little inspiration has come down the generations too. 'I think of the character or creature and how it could be a functional, clever, elegant object … and start doodling & making mock-ups with old cereal packets.'

Spending part of her childhood growing up in Kenya no doubt also had an influence on her enjoyment of using animals in her work – giraffes and their long necks, monkeys in the trees and lions – plenty to excite a child's – and a designer's – imagination. So it does seem rather appropriate that Bryony has been Artist in Residence at Edinburgh Zoo.

> 'I think of the character or creature and how it could be a functional, clever, elegant object … and start doodling & making mock-ups with old cereal packets.'

Based in Coburg House Studios in Leith, she likens her workspace to a den that's also a place of escape. Hand tools, hammers and books for inspiration are laid out nearby so they can be grabbed quickly when needed. The workbench catches the sunlight at 2 p.m. and Bryony enjoys the light streaming in while she sits piercing metal and tap tap tapping with her chasing punches. Past work from her Masters degree, when she was exploring kinetic gates, fills the walls and the rest of the space is full of eclectic ephemera, tin toys and bits and bobs. It's a fascinating space to enter, and so interesting to spend time just looking around, something many people do during Open Studios weekends.

Bryony's latest collection is a series of kinetic silver objects, with function and form inspired by the essence of animals and birds. Her work explores the combination of glass and contemporary chased silver, creating sculptural yet functional silverware with a twist. 'The kinetic element always tickles me. I love it when I show a hidden moving element to a client or onlooker and they giggle or gasp slightly!'

Bryony did a BA (Hons) in Three-Dimensional Design at the University of Wolverhampton, a Masters in Design and Metalwork at Glasgow School of Art (GSA) and then a postgraduate course at Bishopsland. It was while studying in Wolverhampton she first started making automata and was influenced by the work of Paul Spooner and Jean Tinguely, enjoying the interaction, humour and surprise the medium can produce. At GSA she made figurative kinetic gates and Bryony found that metal suited her temperament, being more of a hammerer than a meticulous measurer. She has found the material colourful, magical and malleable and discovered that once you understand how it works you can make it in all scales – from jewellery to weathervanes. 'Most people don't realise how amazing the material of metal is. I love using the rich colours of steel, brass and copper as well as more precious ones.'

Bryony specialises in the ancient silversmithing method of repoussé and chasing: Repoussé is a French term meaning 'pushed up' – a metalworking technique that creates an image in relief on a sheet of metal; chasing is refining the design on the front of the work by sinking the metal. Small, specially shaped punches are used with a hammer to sculpt the desired design. The techniques of repoussé date from antiquity and have been used widely with gold and silver

> 'My work is most satisfying when I have the final piece in my hands, and it looks like the first glimpse I saw in my mind's eye – and then it moves!'

for fine detailed work and with copper, tin and bronze for larger sculptures. Among the most famous classical pieces using this technique are the bronze Greek armour plates from the third century BC and in 1400 BC, the Egyptian Amarna period, resin and mud for repoussé backing was in use. By using her myriad of small steel punches, hammers and chisels, Bryony fashions and forms her exquisite silver sculptures, and feels the strong link to all the past craftspeople who have worked this method before her.

The artistry is clear to see in the commissions that Bryony has created in recent years: a Cockatrice Cocktail Shaker for Asprey; Rhino Hair Comb and Letter-rack presented to HRH Princess Anne from the Royal Zoological Society; Dancing Mice Spectacles Rest for C Marks – to name just a few. There's also a jewellery collection with the most delicious names inspired by nursery rhymes: Sing a Song of Sixpence Ring; Blackbirds in a Pie – Silver Box and Earrings Set; Runcible Spoon Brooches with articulated legs; Silver Sixpence in Your Shoe Wedding Shoe Clip; all testament to a vivid and fun imagination coupled with adroit craftsmanship and design ability. 'Last year I was commissioned to make a silver and gold swan decanter for the Worshipful Company of Vintners. As you poured the wine, the golden beak opened magically. It was the most I had pushed my repoussé and mechanical skills, but I was so pleased with the final result.'

Bryony has made trophies for Red Bull sporting events for the last ten years – crazy things from cliff-diving dragons to Big Ben made from tin cans (an image of which was shown all over the London tube and bus system.) The most unusual commission has to be a life-size 'pointy boob' Madonna-style basque made from Irn-Bru cans for an advert! 'My work is most satisfying when I have the final piece in my hands, and it looks like the first glimpse I saw in my mind's eye – and then it moves!'

Downtime is a sneaky afternoon film at the Cameo cinema with a Bakewell tart and a ginger beer, or a family cycle down the Water of Leith to the Gallery of Modern Art to visit Paolozzi's Studio. There are also visits to Edinburgh Zoo – especially the Pelican Walk, and Dr Neil's Garden in Duddingston, to watch the birds on the water – and everything in the National Museum of Scotland.

This award-winning silversmith is delighted that she can make a (modest) living at something she loves so much. It's taken her abroad to teach and sell in Canada and the US; exhibited at COLLECT (nine times since 2004) in the Saatchi Gallery in London; been part of Bute House Showcase of Scottish Silversmiths, and to exhibit at Goldsmiths' Fair in London and Elements in Edinburgh. This year Bryony has another accolade to add to her CV – that of being one of the participants in BBC Two's *The Victorian House of Arts and Crafts* where she and five other craftspeople are transported back in time to live and experience first hand the ideas and practices of Arts and Crafts visionaries William Morris, John Ruskin and Gertrude Jekyll.

And the future? '2019 will be my twentieth year in business and I'm hoping to celebrate with exciting exhibitions, including COLLECT 2019, commissions and continuing to spread the love of chasing and repoussé. I'd also like to collaborate on some large-scale work with the artisans I met on the BBC series.'

www.bryonyknox.com

Instagram: @bryonyknox
Twitter: @bryonyknox

Hannah Louise Lamb

JEWELLER

A graduate of the Royal College of Art, Hannah Louise Lamb designs and makes jewellery based on coastlines and landscapes, personalised to people's own favourite places.

It was a CDT teacher at school who really inspired and encouraged Hannah towards a creative career. Initially she thought she wanted to be a furniture designer, then a ceramicist. However, when she took an Art Foundation course and for every open project she produced teeny tiny little objects, her tutor suggested she should apply for a jewellery course. A degree in Silversmithing and Jewellery at Glasgow School of Art was followed by a Masters at Royal College of Art.

Originally from Cornwall, Hannah's designing is steeped in the familiar ideas of place and home we can all share, and the inspiration for her jewellery has, in recent years, become focused on the coastlines, vintage maps, colours and textures that draw associations with her idyllic Cornish childhood growing up on the beach, and now her coastal home near Edinburgh. Realising this pull to place and home, Hannah designed the Coastline Collection knowing it would allow people to tell their own stories, capture their memories and encapsulate them in something truly precious to keep and wear.

'Every single piece I make is different as it's tailored to the customer's own favourite map location ... No two pieces are ever the same, and they have such meaning to my customers.'

The process begins with a map or photograph of the desired coastline or landscape that the customer would like. These oblique and asymmetrical shapes and angles are then transferred onto metal in preparation for the next stage. This metal initially comes in sheets and strips, and can be bought at different thicknesses in a range of precious metals. Hannah enjoys using recycled materials like palladium, platinum and gold. At the end of 2018 she became registered to use Fairmined metals. This desire to impact less on the environment is important to the jeweller as well as to her customers and it adds another element to the story behind the work she creates.

The complex map with its intricate shape is then cut out with an extremely fine piercing saw that has a very thin but strong blade. It is a traditional jewellery technique; no lasers are used. The importance of specific tools to artists can never be underrated. Hannah could not be without her saw – it's the one she got in her toolbox when she started at college and it's been used virtually every working day since then. It's been broken and repaired a few times but it's still going strong. Everything else in the toolbox is really old – a second-hand set of tools was acquired when starting out and they all have a satisfying feel and handle perfectly for each task they're needed for. The only new one is the hide mallet used for tapping the rings into a circle. On a working trip to India, Hannah realised that these kind of mallets were impossible to get there, so she left hers behind for the students – it's a consolation that this beloved tool has, no doubt, become very precious to many people many miles away.

Once the sawing is complete the metal is then formed, sanded and polished. Stones can be added – mainly diamonds but sometimes topaz or sapphires. These delicate and precious stones are often used to pinpoint a specific place on a coastline. For Edinburgh to Dunbar for instance, there could be a diamond at North Berwick, a place that will be of personal importance to the customer.

Sometimes Hannah doesn't know the reason for the commission until an email pops in once it's been received. There's often a sentimental connection to the location and Hannah really appreciates when her customers share their personal stories with her. 'Every single piece I make is different as it's tailored to the customer's own favourite map location, and I find

this very inspiring. No two pieces are ever the same, and they have such meaning to my customers. I get to be involved in lots of secret proposals and also sentimental heirlooms, which is a real honour.'

If it's a ring, the coastline is mirrored on the other side and the two pieces are then interlocked together and a circle is created. In the collection there are the rings, of course, and also cufflinks, earrings, bangles, keyrings and necklaces. The stunning coast rings have become the most popular and they are beautiful to behold, especially with a shining precious stone embedded in the gold or platinum. If two tones of gold are used, the matt yellow gold can represent the land and the polished white gold the sea – or vice versa. The wonderful thing is that it's the customer's choice and this is most important to Hannah's work, that the customer receives something unique, original and to their own specifications.

The meaning behind each bespoke piece is important to Hannah and if she knows the story behind it, when she's sawing away, she can't help but think about the narrative associated with it, whether it's a proposal, honeymoon or a favourite walk, and all this emotional creativity is plain to see in her expert skill and craftsmanship in the finished pieces. One of the most popular shorelines is of Iona. Hannah is represented by Aosdana Gallery there, and frequent requests come in for her gorgeous designs to be personalised by specific areas around the Inner Hebridean island.

There's a 'ready to wear' collection too that includes the most popular coastlines as well as pretty 'rolled wave' studs with the satin finish texture and shape emulating the rolling waves and water rippling on the sea. Other earrings are inspired by the patterns of driftwood on the shoreline and have skilfully textured burnished edges that add a bit of sparkle to the finish. There are delicate necklaces that combine the rolling wave motif with pearls or labradorite beads and dark brown braided leather bracelets with interlocking sterling silver coastline hoops.

The skills Hannah employs in making her jewellery are rooted in traditional fabrication techniques and quality workmanship, focusing specifically on intricate hand-piercing and cut-outs. The end result is a stunningly exquisite piece of jewellery – heirloom worthy – that with proper care can be passed down through the family.

Based just outside Edinburgh, Hannah has a 'shedio' – a cross between a shed and a studio – in the garden, and she absolutely loves it. Having moved from a large studio space in Leith, downsizing was needed but with a space designed to her own specifications, it's perfect. The workspace is created from a sleek and practical kitchen unit and worktop with plenty of drawers so that everything can be tucked neatly away. There are large one-off brooches framed and displayed on a shelf and an old printer tray where little bits of inspiration that are found or created are kept until they're ready to be used.

And it's this printer tray of 'itsy' bits that can inform new work, helping her consider new designs. There are pieces that have been used as templates that can be drawn on for fresh approaches, shapes and forms. These materials can spark exciting ideas about what's going to be made in the future. Other inspirations include visits to antique fairs to search out vintage maps, as well as coastal walks, of course. 'I love the east coast, from Edinburgh east to Dunbar via Portobello, Gullane, North Berwick and Aberlady. The beach at Yellowcraigs is perfect for a windy walk and to be inspired by the coastline'.

Ongoing work includes special commissions using some heirloom gold and diamonds to make a coastline wedding ring. Another is a gorgeous inherited stone that's being added to a coast ring. A potential future project is to create a series of one-off large brooches. Hannah sees these as little stand-alone landscapes and would love to design and craft more when there's time.

Hannah's craftsmanship and jewellery-making skills bring her clients from all over the world – whether it's through her online business or referrals from galleries, or meeting potential clients at shows. There's been residencies and led workshops in India and closer to home in the UK, and commissions for The Bodleian Library, The Scottish Government and Scottish Opera, as well as an upcoming trip to participate in a show in New York. 'I still can't believe I went off to art school with no clue where I would end up, somehow graduated with a first, somehow got into the RCA, and then graduated and started setting up a business and earning a living from people wanting to pay for what I want to make? That's an honour!'

She's so busy now that she often has an assistant working with her, but she still keeps all the metal map contour cutting to herself. Like handwriting, her sawing has its own identifiable style and it really gives her work a wonderful 'Hannah Louise Lamb' identity – and, of course, she would not be at all happy handing that well-worn and trusty saw to anyone else.

www.hannahlouiselamb.co.uk

www.facebook.com/hannahlouiselamb
Instagram: @hannahlouiselamb
Twitter: @jewellerylamb

Fiona McIntosh

PRINTED TEXTILE DESIGNER

Tessuti Scotland is the brand name of printed textile designer Fiona McIntosh who has her perfectly shaped studio in the Albion Business Centre to the north-east of the city. Once the Dunbar Lemonade Factory, the building is full of small businesses and artists and very close to the famous Hibernian football ground at Easter Road. Fiona's studio is perfectly shaped because the space was designed around the need for a 7m- long print table – just what's necessary for the screen-printing process she uses to produce her eye-catching and wearable textile collections.

The Scottish College of Textiles, now known as Heriot-Watt School of Textiles and Design, is where Fiona studied for her degree. She enjoyed the very technical course covering weave, knit and print, then spent the final two years specialising in print. Fiona appreciated the almost instant results from that discipline and knew that she had found the medium she wanted to work in.

Although the course was geared to working with established companies in the industry, on graduating in 1984, Fiona and a friend set up Tessuti Scotland together. They started to work with what was a small but vibrant group of fashion designers in Edinburgh. Tessuti would design and print the cloth that the fashion designers would use in their collections. By 1988 Fiona's business partner decided to move to Australia but Fiona kept the brand name, and began concentrating on having her screen-printed cloth manufactured into her own range of accessories.

A huge fan of the imagery, design and colours of the 1950s and '60s, Fiona draws inspiration from these eras to produce her very desirable collections. With such a passion for mid-century design, including vintage ceramics and fabrics, Fiona's colour palette is reminiscent of these tones. Other inspirations include the work of Robin and Lucienne Day in textiles and furniture, and the textile designs of Scottish designer Robert Stewart, who taught at the Glasgow School of Art in the 1970s.

Describing her aesthetic as 'classic with a twist', Fiona has nine styles of scarves in her current collection varying from silk skinnies and squares to large blanket scarves and wraps using Georgette, Crepe de Chine, Silk Habotai, Silk Twill, fine wool and lambswool throughout the range. There's also the exquisite silk 'Ribbony' style of scarf. Initially designed to make sure that all her material was used up, it's now a firm feature in the collection and is

> 'The most enjoyable point is taking the fabric out of the steamer and seeing the results – especially if it's a new print.'

a fabulous example of all her prints and tones sitting beautifully together. All the materials arrive at the studio in their natural base colour of white, cream or ivory and are then hand dyed with acid dyes and printed using the 'discharge' method. Discharge printing is a screen-printing process where, instead of using normal ink, specialised discharge inks are used which remove the dye instead of putting a colour on top of the cloth. The discharge print method of bleaching out a light pattern on a dark background allows Fiona to produce richly hued designs on fabrics whilst retaining their original softness.

Colour is king for Fiona and she mixes all her own dyes and blends away until she manages to find the perfect intense shades for printing. Once printed, the fabric is then dried, steamed, washed, dried again and sent out to be sewn up by a team of locally based outworkers. For every new collection there's a fresh colour palette and print, and a new style of scarf will replace one already in the collection. 'I'm most inspired when trying out a new colourway or print and the most enjoyable point is taking the fabric out of the steamer and seeing the results – especially if it's a new print.'

Fiona doodles and draws constantly in sketchbooks, coming up with print ideas on paper, not on computer, and that gives her work a very distinctive style in today's market. 'For me things are very much the same as they've been in the past because I don't digitally print or use a computer to design. I like the "handmade" look of my work.' An acetate copy is then created of the design she wants to print. All the screens are made up in the workshop and these will be re-used for new designs. In the photographic process of creating the screens, the screen gets a mesh which is coated with light-sensitive emulsion. This is then dried in the dark. The acetate is placed over the treated mesh and an ultraviolet light burns out the marks that have been made. Screen-printing is then the opposite of linocut for instance, in that the marks made are the marks that are printed.

Fiona loves the results she gets from the process of screen printing and can see herself doing it 'as long as she can stand up'! The skill and expertise she brings to the process result in brilliant dramatic patterns of abstract and geometric shapes, in stunning strong colours that sit together beautifully on the soft and tactile luxury materials.

The screen-printing technique has been a vehicle for personal creativity since the method was first used in China around AD 960. However, early forms of stencilling – the printing method required for screen printing – were found in caves in the form of handprints dating back to the prehistoric period and are seen as the earliest form of artistic expression.

Fiona is keen to pass on her expertise and is really proud of the positive feedback that comes after a student has spent time with her in the studio, learning the craft. In some cases it's given the students the confidence to tackle their final year and make decisions about what they would like to specialise in.

Fiona's brand, Tessuti Scotland, has an impressive array of clients both in the UK and in the US. The designs are regularly showcased at UK tradeshows and this has led to the collections being stocked in a range of independent shops and boutiques, museums and galleries. Stockists include The National Galleries of Scotland and the iconic Jenners department store on Princes Street in Edinburgh. And in the US clients include the Freehand Gallery in Los Angeles, the Museum of Design in San Francisco and Ojai in California.

Special commissions have been for corporate clients like the University of Edinburgh and Pringle and there's been superb collaborations with Eribe Knitwear for Urban Outfitters and with Joey D, an Edinburgh-based fashion designer who has a shop on Broughton Street. Fiona and Joey D have now collaborated on a few of his collections, creating fabrics for his clothing

'For me things are very much the same as they've been in the past because I don't digitally print or use a computer to design. I like the "handmade" look of my work.'

line and also upholstery cloth for his furniture range. It might be Harris Tweed or Camouflage fabric and Fiona will be given the print design by Joey D, but then she has carte blanche on colourways and print placing – a fantastic partnership.

Fiona's designs can be found at direct selling events and previous shows have been #Cloth at the Dovecot Gallery in Edinburgh, MADE London and the Craft Scotland Summer Show. US exhibitions have included shows with the American Craft Council in Baltimore, Maryland and the Philadelphia Gift Fair. Both the Baltimore and Philadelphia shows were organised by Craft Scotland, the public body that supports Scotland's craft practitioners in a variety of different ways through events, training and exhibitions of work.

Concrete Wardrobe, the shop Fiona co-owns with fellow textile designer James Donald, also stocks the collection, of course. The business originally started just as a short-term pop-up shop, long before pop-ups became fashionable. The pop-up stocked Fiona and James' work and that of two other local designers. Now Concrete Wardrobe, permanently sited in Broughton Street, is a successful business that specialises in Scottish design-led crafts – created by designers based in or trained in Scotland. The shop has been open for eighteen years and is well known for its high quality, handcrafted designs. It's become a bit of an Edinburgh institution and frequently makes the top ten boutique lists in newspaper and magazines.

For relaxation Fiona enjoys browsing vintage fairs and visiting the Dovecot Gallery, where she loves the atmosphere and the absorbing exhibitions – recent shows have included Liberty Fabrics and Bernat Klein, as well as talks on Jean Muir and the 'Picasso to Warhol' touring exhibition. More inspiration can be found on a walk along Regent Road in Edinburgh from the art deco-influenced building of St Andrew's House, following the road round Calton Hill and enjoying the amazing view out over Waverley Station, the Canongate and Holyrood Park.

www.tessutiscotland.co.uk

www.facebook.com/InfoTessuti
Instagram: @fionamarymcintosh
Twitter: @infotessuti
Concrete Wardrobe, 50A Broughton Street, Edinburgh, EH1 3SA

Choi Keeryong

GLASS ARTIST

'I think I always look for something familiar and unfamiliar – something of the in-between.' When gazing at Choi Keeryong's stunning glass sculptures, they do indeed evoke a feeling of 'unhomeliness' or 'uncanny-ness' which is exactly what the artist is striving for in his work.

He has developed inlaid decorative techniques, inspired by the ancient Korean 'Sanggam' pottery and this allows him to explore the interesting visual reaction from the viewer by defining geometric patterns and counterfeit letters onto the glass and then capturing these patterns between further layers of transparent glass. The result is indeed uncanny as the layers almost appear as if they might be moving, or shimmering, and the optical illusion is emphasised as Choi intertwines the popularity of English ceramic teapots with the historical symbolism of tea and traditional Korean vessels.

'The Korean Glass series I recently created takes the recognisable pattern of the English manufactured porcelain teapot and its forms, and juxtaposes them with counterfeit Korean letters and patterns over the glass body. This questions the authenticity of the object in terms of its cultural origin. Observers in the UK may be familiar with the porcelain elements – but they think of "Korean glass" as an Oriental object because the pseudo-Korean design interrupts the familiarity of the first visual message. Conversely, the counterfeit Korean letters, the patterns on the porcelain, and the Korean viewer's unfamiliarity with glass as an artistic medium, lead audiences there to view the object as "foreign", or as something made by a foreign artist to imitate a Korean object.'

Choi's pioneering process to create one of the Korean Glass series involves blowing a bubble called a blank. Lines and pattern are then drawn onto the blank and once the design is applied and finished, the blank is brought to a small kiln and reheated to 560 degrees. Then a transparent glass is created over the designed blank and once that is cooled down the top surface is then engraved, and this is where the optical illusion is enforced. The cooling down process takes two to three days each time and the creation of each piece is more than three weeks. It's a very long and concentrated process that involves great skill, dexterity and attention to detail.

Choi was born in South Korea and when he was studying in the 1990s there were very few artists working with glass. Only three art colleges offered glass courses, and not even as a degree course, but as part of a metal or ceramic design course. This may be because glass, as an artistic medium, was only introduced to Korea in the 1980s, making it a new and fresh material that Choi wanted to work with.

Glass originally came to Korea through the silk route – via the Middle East, Iraq, India and Asia – but was really introduced into the fabric of Korean society by the Russians as they extended their empire and influence over 150 years ago. There had been a very different appreciation of glass in the East until then as they already had so many well established and more natural materials, so historically, although porcelain ceramics were abundant, there was not much work undertaken with glass.

Because Choi's art college in South Korea did not have a glass course, his tutor invited a glass artist, who studied in Rochester, USA, to introduce the 'new artistic medium' to his students. The artist also brought some foreign glass art books and this introduction was an eye-opening experience for Choi. He immediately wanted to start working with it, his curiosity drawn from the fact that the use of glass in Korea had such a short history relative to its use in the West. However, as there was no art college that would enable him to study for his Master's degree in South Korea using this medium, he moved to Edinburgh to study at the Edinburgh College

of Art under the supervision of Dr Ray Flavell and Alison McConachie, both established glass artists in their own right and whose work Choi enjoyed and admired.

'Although glass in the West, and porcelain in the East, developed under different cultural and historical circumstances, the unique distinctions in both cultures becomes more abstract and blurred as the interplay between the two cultures became more complicated, dynamic and interactive. So, the reason I chose glass and porcelain as my primary materials, and glassblowing as the main means of developing a body of artwork, is to highlight the tensions, conflicts, uncertainty and negotiations which, I believe, are a by-product of the cultural exchanges and unequal relationships between the West and East. Furthermore, my intention in combining the two materials and creating unfamiliar images is to invoke a sense of unhomeliness in viewers, in both the UK and South Korea.'

The glassmaking process requires the artist to have acquired a certain level of skill to achieve a satisfactory result in the studio. The results of the glassmaking cannot be predetermined, but it largely, or wholly, depends on the artist's judgement, dexterity and care throughout the delicate process. Learning glassmaking, therefore, can be characterised as a constant negotiation between the artist and the artistic medium of glass, in order to achieve the best possible outcome from the making process.

For Choi's most recent project, he intended to learn and embrace all the challenges involved in the process, including the failures that influence achieving the best possible results. To do that, Choi deliberately chose to create bubbles on the casted glass surface. Bubbles are often regarded as a failure for glass artists, but by using small frit size glass and skipping the bubble soaking process during the kiln firing, he has made them a feature of his new work. However, by applying gold-leaf inlay on the bubbles, he is also celebrating their instability and uniqueness.

This new work, entitled the Daam Dah series, meaning 'to embrace' or 'layer', are sculptural works informed by bringing circle and square together along three-dimensional lines. For Choi this work doesn't have any particular cultural influence but still plays with the ideas of familiar and unfamiliar that underpins his work. When Choi feels that his work looks like something that doesn't belong, he knows it is now ready to create. The finished pieces can be seen as beautiful sculptured works of art to be enjoyed for their design and form, and the beauty of the process, but these are also closed objects with lids so there is always the possibility that something could be inside, again leading the viewer to question the meaning and veracity of what they see.

'I am hoping my work can provoke some awareness of many issues that are constructed around cross-cultural experiences.'

Choi describes his studio space as small but cosy, dark but comfortable, and cold enough to keep him awake! The workspace has an industrial feel to it but the delicate objects sitting around his studio also seem to replicate the contrasts in his work. There is a mixture of very fine and large industrial tools hooked on the wall, and crowded shelves indicate all the different elements of his process. Choi tends to work alone in his studio, enjoying the solitude when making but appreciating the proximity of other artists when he can, finding inspiration in conversations about alternative disciplines and approaches to processes and ideas. 'I am hoping my work can provoke some awareness of many issues that are constructed around cross-cultural experiences.'

His workshop is based in Leith and this is another area of influence for Choi with the intermingling of cultures and a rather chaotic mix of shops: smells from the Chinese supermarkets and Indian takeaway restaurants; the African barbershop and the unfamiliar lettering on a package from the Polish supermarket. One can understand why the artist would feel comfortable with the feelings of the familiar and unfamiliar that the local area brings.

Choi is encouraged by the reactions to his work and enjoys developing a body of artwork that examines the feelings of unease evoked when viewing the glass pieces. He likes to understand an individual's consumption of the artwork and their aesthetic experiences with it. Therefore, the distinctive qualities of Choi's work rely on the sense of bicultural identity present within.

Once Choi completed his Masters he embarked on a PhD in Glass and Architectural Glass. He has exhibited widely across the UK whilst investigating the similarities and differences between cultural groups in terms of their aesthetic perceptions of visual experiences, particularly in relation to unfamiliar materials and surface imagery.

The National Museum of Scotland purchased Choi's work *Korean Glass 15 (2013)* last year. 'As a Korean artist trained and based in Scotland, my work being included in the Museum's collection means a lot to me.' Choi has also exhibited at the London Design Fair under the Craft Scotland banner, and at the Scottish Gallery Edinburgh, as well as throughout the UK and further afield.

Instagram: @choi_keeryong_glass

Robin Abbey

TRADITIONAL SIGNWRITER AND GILDER

Robin Abbey developed a passion for lettering from a very young age, creating posters as a child amateur, copying letters out of newspapers or from book covers. 'I would copy the headlines from the paper, and whilst still at school in Bridgwater, Somerset, painted a placard, which read "Farm Workers demand £7 now" for the annual Martyrs Rally at Tolpuddle!'

Coming from a farming background, Robin's parents wanted him to get a 'proper job' but he saw art college as the next best thing and followed his early passion to gain a City & Guilds in Typographic Design at Somerset College of Art. Various jobs in different aspects of printing, proofreading and graphic design followed but he always did some form of lettering in the evenings and at weekends. A lifestyle change following recovery from bipolar disorder brought him to Edinburgh in 1999 and he's been working in the city as a traditional signwriter ever since.

Describing his craft as 'the design and execution of lettering and related matter on painted surfaces, glass and stone', he's seen many changes in his particular field since he began his career. Nowadays, if the skill of a traditional signwriter, like Robin, isn't being used then signage is usually created from a digital design program using typefaces as their base. These are then laser cut from self-adhesive vinyl, taken to site and applied. In the pre-computer era, when Robin was first starting out, and not yet a signwriter, things were very different.

A slide projector would be used with Letraset typography, displayed to the desired height and then traced onto translucent paper. This was traced back onto the wood or acrylic and the letters would all be cut out individually, using a jigsaw. Then they had to be filed to the exact shape. This lettering would be attached to fascia board or wherever they were needed. It was time-consuming and very expensive compared to today's methods. Although many would prefer to use vinyl for their signs and do everything digitally, Robin has constantly had a full workload since he started his business, with clients preferring to go down the traditional route using a skilled artisan. He finds it inspiring knowing that every job, irrespective of size, is contributing to the future security of the craft. He's also very supportive with his time and knowledge, encouraging those who want to learn.

'There's been a tremendous revival of interest in traditional hand-produced lettering in the last five years or so. I'm glad to be part of it and able to pass on my skills.'

Working out of a large space in Coburg House Studios (Robin, of course, created the magnificent exterior signage for the studios) he describes his studio as 'teetering on the edge of chaos'! It's a real treasure trove where you could easily while away an hour just browsing through. Examples of lettering, gilding and glass-work are on the worktops and leaning against the walls; various signage of different colours and styles are dotted around the room and an old Imperial typewriter sits just waiting to be used. One wall is covered in tools including various size saws and hammers; there's a bookcase with a library devoted to his favourite subject; sheets of wood and lots and lots of specialist paints and sizes. (Size is a liquid applied to a painting surface such as canvas, wood or paper used to fill the pores of the fibres and seal the surface to make it less absorbent.)

However, it's an organised chaos and testament to how popular his expertise is. Robin does combine some new technology with his craft. Logos, for example, can be emailed to him in PDF form. These are expanded to the desired size and then one of the oldest techniques is used, one that Michelangelo utilised, and that's perforating the outlines of the text with a little spiked wheel called a pounce wheel. The tiny perforations are then dusted through with French chalk and a ghostly outline is revealed which is then filled in with the appropriate paint. Despite all this, basic traditional signwriting consists of setting out by eye the desired wording with chalked strap-lines to indicate the positions of the letters, and shading if required. The paint is then applied, or size if gold leaf is required. It's a simple process, but one that could only be done successfully by someone with years of experience.

Often a couple of days prep is needed before actually going to the location and creating the sign, depending on how much new design work is needed. Sometimes the shape of letters needs to be altered slightly to make the spacing come right and Robin has found that roman and block lettering in particular will withstand a lot of stretching and squashing. The trick is to compensate as you go along to make the final work look perfect.

Clients range from domestic customers wanting numerals over their house door to a new restaurant looking for a dynamic sign to herald their presence. Gilding new names onto honours boards for organisations and clubs is very popular – in fact, in one Masonic Lodge, the work has been going on for so long that it's like a history of signwriting, seeing the same style of lettering done in slightly different ways by various signwriters as the years have gone by.

Gilding needs a lot of expertise, with timing being an important element in the whole process. Oil-based size is used in the place of paint. Sizes dry at different speeds, the speed relating to the time is takes before it gets to the perfect tackiness for the next stage. Outside, for instance, you would want a pretty fast speed, especially if you're dealing with changeable Edinburgh weather! Once the right consistency, or tack, is achieved, the gold leaf is applied. Leaf is supplied by Wrights of Lymm in 3-inch squares, each piece attached to a transfer sheet for exterior use. The gold is very fine – 0.134 microns. It's smoothed onto the sized areas, and the excess is gently taken off with cotton wool, leaving clean, sharp edges. Burnishing the surface (polishing gently with cotton wool) can add a lustre to the finished lettering but is not always desirable.

Robin couldn't do his work without his mahlstick and selection of paintbrushes. The mahlstick is generally thought of as something the painter rests their hand on while using the paintbrush but in actual fact, Robin uses both hands to co-ordinate the movement. The 'writer' paintbrush is the workhorse of signwriters. It's chisel-shaped and with different pressures can give a variety of results. A 'rigger' brush is traditionally used for copperplate lettering and apparently developed for painting rigging on ships. This brush can be charged with paint and allows a long perfect line to be drawn without having to refresh the paint – Robin has got straight lines down to 1mm! Flat head brushes are used for italics. Sword liners, introduced from the US, are used for coach lines and pin striping.

Robin has his own favourite styles of lettering – he finds traditional Roman a real pleasure to produce and sometimes when there's a rare quiet time in all the busy-ness in the studio, he will paint a Roman 'S' for the sheer pleasure of doing it. 'Perpetua is also lovely to paint. Gill Sans easy to do; designed by Eric Gill who was an artist originally, you can almost feel where his pencil has been. If in doubt – Gill throughout!'

'You call on all the styles of lettering you have memorised and then play on variations of them. Just like a jazz musician, the more experience you have the more and better you can play.'

Since the advent of the computer, people have become familiar with typefaces and assume that fonts are being used. To Robin fonts are like sheet music whereas signwriting is like jazz. 'You call on all the styles of lettering you have memorised and then play on variations of them. Just like a jazz musician, the more experience you have the more and better you can play.'

Robin enjoys working on location just as much as his studio work, although it's not without its pitfalls. Using ladders on a main street can be quite precarious, especially when so many people are looking at their mobile phones and do not see the ladders. Other times people watch him work, enjoying the beauty of it and the evident skill.

His work can be seen all around Edinburgh, and further afield. He's particularly proud that he's been doing all the signwriting for Maxies Bistro in Edinburgh for over ten years. The Cutting Room and The Cat's Miaou on Leith Walk, The Raging Bull on Lothian Road and The Signet Library in Parliament Square have all used Robin's craftsmanship. Clients come back time and again and he's also sought after by other artisans – Mackenzie Leather, Hannah Louise Lamb, James Donald and Bryony Knox, all featured in this book, have happily used his services.

Relaxation involves strolling around the New Town, enjoying the beautifully planned streets, the architecture and the general Georgian grandeur – and the coffee. Occasionally he can still identify the original painted street names in white on black, which, of course, are particularly appealing. Rowing at Port Seton Coastal Rowing Club, the occasional foray to a pub for a singsong and reading all occupy many happy leisure hours.

The future involves a continually busy workload of all different kinds of commissions but Robin wouldn't have it any other way, and the variety keeps things interesting. As long as there's also time to pass on his skills in some way he's happy, and he's looking forward to doing more tutoring both in his studio and at West Dean College in Sussex. The best part of his work is when Robin has completed a well-proportioned sign then watching the client's face on first seeing it – taking pleasure in the craftsmanship on display.

www.robinabbeysignwriting.co.uk
Instagram: @robinabbey1

Peter Holmes

UPHOLSTERER AND FURNITURE MAKER

Peter Holmes is an upholsterer and furniture maker with over thirty years' experience. He originally trained in Lancaster, starting his own business at the age of 20. However, after five years Peter was bitten by the travel bug and journeyed through South East Asia, Australia and New Zealand, using his upholstery skills along the way. A few years working in London followed, before travelling again, this time in East and Southern Africa and on returning to the UK, Peter settled in Edinburgh.

In 2000 Peter took on Be Seated. The business specialises in producing bespoke upholstered furniture along with the restoration of antique pieces; his specialty being post-war 'mid-century' furniture. 'It's the quality, the design, the ergonomic shape and form. It's all there in this period of furniture. The frames of the pieces are built to last. They are so beautifully made, just wonderful craftsmanship.'

Post-war Europe and the UK were heavily influenced by the post-Bauhaus school of design, with the Scandinavians at the forefront of combining beautiful organic frames and an excellent quality of fabric with muted tones. Some of this work was mass produced but not to the point where quality was compromised, the frames solid and hand-finished, utilising new and traditional fillings to bring modern shape and form to a much wider post-war customer base. British design was in turn influenced by Scandinavian design, and British designers, like Robin and Lucienne Day, combined this and the post-Bauhaus influence into their progressive shapes and fabric patterns that inspire Peter and his work.

Peter embraces traditional techniques but is not a purist, working in every way possible to extend the longevity of the designs at the same time as embracing their period features. 'My passion is to sympathetically restore these pieces for the future.' Traditional by-product horsehair is sometimes used as well as coconut fibres, or a combination of the two. There are sophisticated new foams that are so much better than some of the conventional ones used in the past. Sometimes these foams can be more expensive but are longer lasting and can have a better finish. Often safer and quicker, using them can speed up the process, opening up restoration to a wider audience. Clients don't often realise that upholstery is not just about re-covering in a different fabric, but it's rebuilding the piece from the frame up, taking into account the function as well as the form.

Responsive restoration involves the thoughtful selection of the new fabric to be used as well. It's important to spot fabric trends but also to remember how long the piece of furniture is intended to last; that the style is classic and the materials must match that. It's this attention to detail that brings many furniture dealers to Peter; they are appreciative of his sensitivities and know the workmanship and craft will be considered and complementary. Sofas and chairs will be sold on to collectors and the fabric used must be able to sustain in their new environment. Peter mostly uses wool and other natural fibres like linen and cotton. These materials have the best stretch and are long lasting. For special projects, hand-loomed cloth can be used to add a further bespoke style element to the restoration of a period piece. Occasionally some work is outsourced, like cabinetry or machinist work, and Peter often brings in apprentices to whom he can pass his skills on and to help keep the craftsmanship alive. The last few trainees have been women, making a welcome entry into what has been mostly a male domain historically.

The Be Seated workshop is on a busy main road in the Leith area of Edinburgh and the windows always have wonderful examples of Peter's work so that passers-by can stop and admire. You can also see the showroom further back, currently full of stunning pieces including a newly restored Sampsel sofa by Carl Malmsten. One of Peter's admired mid-century designers, Malmsten championed craft-based furniture design, based on local materials and traditions that could be made available to a wider clientele at an affordable price. His work has been described in ecological and sustainable terms, so important to Peter, and the timeless quality of it means that it's as much loved today as in the past. Peter's clients enjoy his expert knowledge of this period of design – and his ability to make it work in a contemporary setting.

Beside the Be Seated showroom is an anteroom that holds hundreds of fabric books and swatches, emphasising Peter's knowledge of the materials he works with and also the size of the choice that's available to customers. Next door is the actual workspace – bright and airy like the

showroom with large windows spilling in lots of light. A considerable variety of specialist and everyday tools hang on the walls and there's a wingback armchair, currently being restored, lying on the work table. Tools range from the traditional magnetic hammer (used alongside magnetic tacks that are held in the mouth and transferred to the hammer as each one is needed); to compressed air staple guns more often used on contemporary designs. There's also an array of very large needles used for a variety of upholstery tasks from slip-stitching to tufting. The rest of the studio holds frames and foams and there's a small office area – all leaving one with the impression of industry and organisation.

Peter does create his own range of furniture and a small collection can be found on his website. These can be made up from the frames he's designed and then upholstered to order. There are collaborations from time to time too, most recently with local furniture designer Namon Gaston when they were commissioned to create a piece, the Oxbow Armchair, for Design Exhibition Scotland. 'Whether restoring or making a piece of furniture, my aim is to provide resolute construction and ergonomically sound furniture.'

Customers who come in after seeing the wonderful selection through the window are usually keen on commissioning a bespoke piece of furniture. Peter likes to sit down with the client and discuss their requirements and budget. 'It's important to listen to their ideas and take note of any concerns such as whether they have any physical issues that might impact on the final design or restoration. The comfort and ergonomics of a piece can vary from client to client, therefore I work closely with my clients to achieve the best possible result.'

'When restoring a family's heirloom piece I want to embrace the emotional connection for the family and make sure it lives on.'

The commissions can range from a hotel ordering a 4m-long sofa (a job that needed its own workbench created to complete it), to having a favourite chair brought back to life. Peter finds that being trusted to restore a family heirloom is a privilege, and is one of the most enjoyable aspects of his work, especially when clients have a sentimental attachment to a particular piece. Knowing the client is putting complete trust in him to restore their piece sympathetically gives Peter great pleasure in his work. Clients appreciate his knowledge of furniture and being able to tell customers the background to their piece – a Chesterfield, for instance – gives them confidence in both him and his work as he talks them through the restoration process. 'When restoring a family's heirloom piece I want to embrace the emotional connection for the family and make sure it lives on.'

Since moving to Edinburgh, Peter enjoys living with the amazing local architecture, art galleries and museums, not to mention the annual arts festival, but what really inspires him is the large collection of small creative businesses in the area that are thriving all around him. This community comes together and collaborates and shares expertise, with everyone benefitting from the support. It's not the easiest thing to be able to live by your own craft work but Peter is really proud that his business is going so well. 'I've had my own business for the best part of twenty-five years so I guess I must be doing something right!'

www.beseated.co.uk

Be Seated 35–37 Ferry Road Edinburgh EH6 4AF
www.facebook.com/BeSeatedLeith
Instagram: @beseatedleith
Twitter: @beseatedleith

Rebecca Wilson

JEWELLER AND CERAMICIST

When you walk into Rebecca Wilson's studio you would be forgiven for thinking you may have entered a sweet shop as her work is inspired by the confectionery industry and a nostalgia for the sweet treats of her childhood.

Rebecca originally studied ceramics to Masters level, first at Duncan of Jordanstone in Dundee then completing her Masters at Cardiff. She enjoyed a decade-long exhibiting career before taking a break from making to start a family. Exhibitions most notably included COLLECT in the Saatchi Gallery, London and at SOFA in Chicago, the Triennial Museum of Art and Design in Milan, and JOYA in Barcelona. However, after a couple of years with less studio time, Rebecca felt it might be a step backwards to pick up where she left off, so took some evening classes in jewellery and subsequently introduced metalwork and wearables to her practice. 'My aim is to glamorise the simple joys in life, celebrating humble pleasures and elevating them to the status of art objects.'

Rebecca's jewellery collection is a rainbow spectrum of sweet treats, from fruit chews and lollies to cakes and pastries piled with cream and icing, distilled down to their simplest forms and married with a sickly sweet colour palette. From earrings, necklaces, brooches and statement pieces, the pastel tones influenced by the sticky opacity of fruity chews, marshmallows and foams are achieved through a combination of softly coloured porcelain and carefully matched gemstones, all wrapped up in silver settings. A wealth of form and pattern is inspired by factory-produced pressed and cast candies, and similarly in the plastic casings that cocoon them. The formality of precious materials is removed to create wearables that drip with the desire of momentary self-indulgence and look good enough to eat, and with titles like Bakewell Tart and Iced Gems, they are very tempting.

The process of creating these wearable works of art always starts with the ceramics that are cast from pieces of plastic packaging. Often Rebecca will buy things that she doesn't really want to eat, but the shape of the treat is perfect for creating a mould for her work – also difficult to do with two young children who may well want the treats for themselves!

Using slip casting, an industrial process that has been used for the mass production of ceramics for centuries, the designer works with it in a scaled-down and intimate way to create short runs of multiples in porcelain. Accents of colour are sometimes added during the casting process, or layered and incised into the surface of the model after it has been removed from the mould. The porcelain clay is stained so subtly that before firing it appears white, and it's only when everything comes out of the kiln that the colours become evident. Ceramics can be a cruel mistress – very occasionally things can come out slumped or with air bubbles –

nothing can be done but to discard it all and move on. After a successful firing, the next stage is the most immersive, laying out and rearranging the porcelain forms and making plans for the new collection.

With a collage of porcelain pieces, silver fittings and stones spread out in front of her, Rebecca will then decide what will go together, moving things around to see how elements will connect. It usually starts with a little bit of everything but gradually ingredients are pared back until the right combination is left and the collection reveals itself.

Decisions then need to be made about the metalwork – is it a claw or bezel setting? Is this a pendant or earring? How can everything be put together without the silver becoming too dominant and imposing as the ceramic needs to be the main feature? Rebecca likes to sketch what's been laid out as she goes along, tracing the outlines of the shapes, and snapping with a camera phone as she works. This fast-paced process allows her to make multiple changes whilst remembering and revisiting earlier versions of each design. She can have up to twenty compositions in progress on her bench at any one time, and when each design is finalised it will be snapped or sketched, then its component parts are filed away in an array of plastic containers to be assembled in turn. Even at this stage things can change, and as a process-led maker, each design can continue to evolve throughout the making process.

'I've always loved the interplay of seemingly incongruous materials. My favourite part of the process is the experimentation stage; working out what new materials are capable of, repurposing objects meant for other applications and making them into jewellery.'

Playing and working with these materials all takes place in a little mint green 'shedio' at the bottom of the garden, all beautifully kitted out inside with a small kiln, large high table, and daylight overhead lighting. 'It's far enough removed from home that I can take myself away from domestic distractions, but close enough that I can commute in my slippers! Pegboard is my friend, and also lots of small drawers. I like to be able to rearrange my space depending on what I am working on, so that all of my tools are close to hand. I also get very excited about tools, and I like to compose them on the walls where I can admire them. I tend to stick with clay at one end of the studio, and silver at the other, because they are both grubby processes that generate incompatible messes. So, one end has

stacks of moulds, boxes of found objects and plastic packaging waiting to be made into moulds, buckets of slip, and jars of fettling tools, sponges and scrapers. The other end has many, many tiny drawers filled with stones, tubes, wires, threads and findings, and a little soldering station made from a repurposed vintage dressing table.'

The studio desk will often be strewn with random objects, from porcelain nuggets in various shapes and sizes, and multi-coloured gemstones, to plastic parts from the automotive industry, biscuit box inserts, sweet wrappers, plastic toys pillaged from the front of children's comics; some are cast to make moulds, some used for mark-making, and others incorporated into the final collection. 'I have great fun collaging with a multitude of small objects to make elaborate compositions, but also find great satisfaction in paring these compositions back, distilling down the essential elements to the point of minimalism.'

Rebecca's first point of inspiration is always the local ice-cream parlour – Luca's. It's a decades-old family-run institution, which is inspiring in itself, and a haven of retro atmosphere, with a vast spectrum of delicious and colourful ice creams and good old-fashioned truffles on offer. There's also Moffat Toffee Shop in the Scottish Borders. A sweet shop with all the old-fashioned

confectioner's jars, unchanged for years: Gumballs; Sherbet Pips; Soor Plooms; Sweet Potatoes – they're all there.

Continuing on the same theme, a new range of pseudo-functional sherbet bowls are planned. These silver-rimmed bowls in pastel-coloured porcelain will recreate specific iconic childhood delicacies. Firstly, the Double Dip, with its two choices of sherbet in pink cherry and orange, and the iconic yellow lozenge-shaped dabber to dip and lick. And secondly, the sherbet Dip Dab, with its fine ice-white powder, luscious red lollipop, recreated using a large ruby set in silver. The ability to get the right shape and colour of the current and planned collections can't be underestimated. The joyful results come from much experimentation, skilled craftsmanship and a playful imagination.

A typical day will involve dropping the kids at nursery and school before making a coffee and heading down the garden to the studio. Rebecca likes to leave something unfinished from the day before and a 'two-song' tidy will begin – any longer would be procrastination – before starting something fresh and finishing from the previous session. There's usually three or four things on the go at once and eventually these will combine to go into the kiln at the same time. Rebecca will be working away on her designs until it's time to pick up the children again and head back home. Working in this way gives her a good life/work balance and she's proud of the fact that she's managed to have a career in making without a break since graduation. Like any designer/maker, it's tough at times juggling everything but the fact that she's managed to maintain a studio and work constantly for fifteen years she puts down to stubborn resilience.

The future involves more international shows and events with exhibitions coming up in Amsterdam and Barcelona. Creatively, plans are also afoot for more statement pieces and a collection inspired by the unassuming Swizzle Stick and Flying Saucers – something we know for sure will look good enough to eat.

www.rebeccawilsonceramics.com

www.facebook.com/RebeccaWilsonCeramics
Instagram: @reb_wilson
Twitter: @RWCeramics

Simon Harvey-Potts

LEATHER ARTISAN

When Simon Harvey-Potts graduated from a film and photography degree and took some time off to go travelling, he had no idea that he would return with a brand new career and an enduring passion that's turned into a successful and thriving business.

Excelling in art at school and very keen on craft Simon knew that his future would be creative, but it was his visit to Spain and in particular Andalucia and Granada that altered the future that he had originally envisaged. He came across local leather artisans and was extremely impressed by their craftwork, knowledge and skill. The Spanish artisans were generous with their knowledge and expertise. They gave Simon his first tools and showed him basic techniques, also pointing him in the direction of where to buy leather hides. It was simple, traditional-style leatherwork: hand stitching and carving, but he discovered a real passion for it, falling in love with the craft. He soaked up as much knowledge as he could and created simple designs. Simon then continued to travel through Spain, France and Italy, and found that he could sell his leather products in markets. This meant he could survive and continue to travel, keeping the European adventure going as well as working with his leather.

Returning to Edinburgh, Simon persevered with his self-education, reading books like *The Art of Hand Sewing Leather* by American leatherwork pioneer Al Stohlman, and *The Leatherworking Handbook* by Valerie Michael. Honing his craft and selling his work in local Edinburgh markets, this was a really enjoyable and happy time but it was a way of working that would only ever just

support him and he wanted more. Simon visited Mackenzie Leather, a local shop on Victoria Street in the Old Town that had become a bit of an Edinburgh institution. Starting the business in the Isle of Arran, Mackenzie opened an Edinburgh shop in 1990 and it was twelve years after that that Simon joined them. He worked part-time initially, having pestered them repeatedly for a job. He had to re-learn some skills as the process was quite different from the way he had been taught in Spain, but he had confidence in what he was doing and the craftsmanship came quickly. After an eight-month apprenticeship and intensive learning in how to make a sporran, book bag and briefcase, he became workshop leader, learning how to make many of the other designs on the job. Eight years passed and the opportunity to take over came when the owner retired. With a helpful push from his fiancée, Simon bought the business on the prophetic date of 11.11.11.

He wanted to keep the heritage of Mackenzie, so didn't change the name, but he closed the shop and took a studio space for five years, perfecting his craft and his own designs. Simon exhibited his work at all the big Scottish shows: Scone Palace, Glamis Castle, The Royal Highland Show and the West End Show. Then, in 2017, Simon opened up a shop back in the heart of the Old Town in St Mary's Street, where the business is located today. It's an ideal position, just off the Royal Mile and perfect for tourists and local residents alike. The traditional entranceway opens into the showroom with the workshop, where you can clearly see everything being made in the back of the store. 'Now, seven years later, I've returned Mackenzie to its rightful place in the heart of the Old Town with a fantastic team and a thriving shop!'

The showroom has an excellent selection of his designs: sumptuous Gladstone bags, book bags, saddle bags and cartridge bags, the business tote, alongside belts, wallets, sporrans and more, all wonderfully put together, with exquisite workmanship, contemporary and traditional designs, and the most tactile leather with a fabulous colour palette to choose from.

Beyond the showroom you can see Simon and his colleagues at work. With the Mackenzie name Simon also inherited the tools and the machinery. The skiving machine (used to shave the edges of leather and make it thinner and easier to work with – this process can also be done by hand) is over 100 years old; the Japanese sewing machine is from the 1960s – machines that are strong and sturdy, built to last. There's a large cutting table, a bell skiver and a wonderful array of well-worn traditional tools, also over 100 years old. The tools now feel like an extension of Simon's hands and he's not sure if he could get the same results from new ones. They're irreplaceable and occasionally he has nightmares about breaking them, of having to replace handles which are just perfect as they are.

'I've returned Mackenzie to its rightful place in the heart of the Old Town with a fantastic team and a thriving shop!'

In the workshop, there's a wall covered in leather ready to be used. Simon works with Italian and Spanish hides that are vegetable tanned, an ancient method of preserving skins. This leather ages fantastically well, the skin gets better with age and you can see the journey of a bag or product evolving over time. The signs of wear and use are particular to the owner, giving an individual connection to what will be a much-loved accessory. Other processes, chrome tanning for instance, can lose any distinction and become bland and lifeless, a complete contrast to the veg tan method. The tannery Simon works with in Spain dates back five generations and they have giant barrels that do the vegetable tanning that he loves. The Italian veg tan leather is heavy and the Spanish light in weight and he enjoys working with both types. Another difference between the two is the finish: the Spanish use oils and wax, whereas in Italy they use fat. Colour, weight and finish – three complementary elements that can be used in different ways in the finished work. 'I really enjoy all aspects of what I do but the beginning process of cutting out the bags and preparing all the components – I always get excited and potentially quite over optimistic as I generally cut out more than we can make in the time given – I am passionate, I guess.'

Great satisfaction in the process of leatherwork comes from the manipulation of the whole hide and cutting the different parts of it for the various components of the bag. Simon loves the tactility of working with the skin, and the mental and physical challenge involved. He can switch off the outside everyday noise, get into a meditative state and work with frantic excitement cutting out what he's going to be making. It's also during this process that new ideas come into his head – perhaps new designs, or a fresh approach to a traditional style. For Simon, it's not easy to sum up, this time of private meditation when working in such a concentrated state, but it's certainly one of the most rewarding stages of the process.

The iconic tool for cutting leather is the Round Leather Cutting Knife, also known as Half Moon or Head Knife. This is the oldest and most traditional tool for cutting and shaping all grades of leather. It's a tool that's been used since Neolithic times and shows how little the tools and process of this ancient craft have changed. In that period it would have been made from flint and used to scrape the back of hides, now it's used more for shaping belts and the thinning down of the leather by hand.

Once the initial cutting has been made, the bags are then put together with a mixture of hand stitching and machine work. The hardware is riveted into position, straps have the edges bevelled, smoothed and stained, handles placed in position. All the other elements that make a bag are carried out by hand, with outstanding craftsmanship evident at each stage of the process. Bags and other accessories from the main collections are made in limited edition runs of about fifteen at a time.

Besides offering a ready-to-buy collection of leather accessories for men and women, Mackenzie also does bespoke orders, customisation and restoration. The extremely popular leather tote bag can be created in different colours for the bag and the handles. It's wonderful that it's possible to go into a shop in a city centre and pick a style one likes with customisation of size, colour, etc. With so many tourists visiting Edinburgh customers come from all over, in particular the US and Canada, Germany, Switzerland and Sweden. You can order while you holiday in Edinburgh and the bag or briefcase or whatever your choice will follow you home. You know that it will be handmade in that workshop, with excellent skill. Bespoke is a large part of the business and one of Simon's favourite things to do.

Simon enjoys sketching out new ideas for the collection. With three staff now working with him, and demand high, it's often too hectic to take advantage of these snatched moments for new work. Designs teamed with waxed cottons from Dundee-based Halley Stevensons have brought a new element to his collection and Simon loves how well the heritage of that company and their product sits with his leatherwork.

From that first travelling experience in Spain, this artisan's career has come a long way. Mackenzie Leather recently won Best Craft Business in the Scottish Business Awards. Simon is really proud of the fact that he's brought Mackenzie back to the city centre where it belongs and now has staff that he can pass on his skills to. For him it's about keeping the tradition and the skills alive and being able to offer the opportunity to others to learn leatherwork in the same way he did when he started out.

When he took Mackenzie Leather over, Simon revisited Granada where it all started and found it a very emotional return, looking down on the area where he first started selling his leatherwork. His commitment, passion and love for the craft shine through and are immediately evident in the accessories he creates, each one a work of art in itself.

www.mackenziebags.co.uk

www.facebook.com/mackenziebags
Instagram: @mackenzieleathergoods

Sally-Ann Provan

DESIGNER/MILLINER

From the Edinburgh Hat Studio, award-winning designer/milliner, Sally-Ann Provan, creates distinctive, elegant, modern millinery. Based at Beaverhall Studios, another creative hub in the centre of Edinburgh, the Hat Studio is a large sunny space with a showroom/shop area at the front with displays of hats that clients can try on or buy. The studio/making area is at the back – closely resembling a tantalising treasure chest with an abundance of feathers and fabrics everywhere, mixed with other hat-making accoutrements.

In her final year of an honours degree in Jewellery and Metalwork at Duncan of Jordanstone College of Art, Sally-Ann started making headdresses and although she enjoyed enamelling and decorative repoussé work she wanted to work with larger and softer materials. As a member of Scotland's Youth Theatre, she had thoroughly enjoyed the costume aspect and had thought about that as a career. However, after a mixed media first year foundation course in Carlisle, she ended up choosing jewellery. Now Sally-Ann feels that her early loves of jewellery and costume have come together with a beautiful serendipity to create her striking collections. With a retired cabinetmaker father and a grandmother who was a confectioner, making delicate sugar roses and icing wedding cakes, it's not at all surprising that the designer is able to step seamlessly from creating delicate flowers for a bridal hat to working on giant illuminated tricornes for a stage production.

After graduating, Sally-Ann had the design experience but needed more technical skills to further her career in the direction she wanted to go. To this end she nurtured her passion with more millinery training – learning the craft with HM the Queen Mother's milliner, the late Mitzi Lorenz, and at the British School of Millinery. She also learned theatrical millinery at the Royal Opera House in Covent Garden and with the prestigious Jane Smith. Now, twenty years on, and running a successful business, she still enjoys learning new techniques, experimenting, and offering a bespoke service designing headwear for events, weddings, garden parties and racing, as well as for opera, ballet, theatre, and television.

'My process is quite a holistic one, I work "in the round" developing ideas by working on a vintage poupeé head called Betty. I do very little drawing – I log ideas and prototypes by taking photos with my phone – these are my sketches. I have a large collection of hat blocks, some are vintage, some made for me, and others that I've made myself – so I quite often start with shape, then colour, then experiment with trimmings. It's all about achieving a balance in the finished piece.'

The hats are all made using a traditional process called blocking – a process used for hundreds of years, where you shape a material by hand using steam over a mould. Many of the materials are traditional too – felts and straws – but new materials and modern technologies are also incorporated into the wonderful compositions. The straw used is mainly sinamay – a material that's woven from fibres of the Abaca plant – a species very similar to the banana palm and native to the Philippines. It's three times stronger than cotton or silk, so it's really durable and long lasting. Many kinds of plant fibres are used – paper straws from China, panamas from Equador, sisal, viscose and bamboo – they all behave differently when steamed and it's Sally-Ann's knowledge, through experimentation and prototyping, that informs the selection of which material to use for which style of hat.

The best hat blocks are made from wood that's been shaped especially for the design that is desired. The expertise is in the manipulation of the materials on the block while steaming, working free-form, stretching and moving the felt or straw to create the shape. As soon as the steaming has stopped and the materials have cooled down, they're firmly set in that form, ready for the next stage. If it's a pillbox hat for instance, the headfitting ribbon, made from grosgrain or petersham, is shaped and sewn inside, and this is fitted to match the dimensions of the wearer. A fedora or a trilby is created in two pieces with the crown blocked first and then the brim. The headfitting ribbon is again used inside, making sure that the measurements are accurate to fit the head perfectly.

> 'I meet a diversity of ladies from all walks of life, and for me it's about finding that balance of shape, colour and trim that brings out their personality.'

Next stage is the decoration, known as trimming, and this is where all the artistry and craft learned as a jeweller can come into play with the use of laser cutting, acrylics or resins and silver- or gold-plated wire teased adroitly into place. Gold leaf, leather, silks, mother of pearl – a whole range of different textures can be used in the finished design. During the trimming process Sally-Ann will model the hat in the mirror – does it need more? Or less? Is it balanced?

Gradually the headwear will be completed and ready for the client.

The materials themselves are a constant source of inspiration and Sally-Ann enjoys working with colour and texture, permitting herself time to 'play' and experiment with ideas – allowing creativity to flow is very important for moving her ideas forward. A few years ago a large laser-cut acrylic head-piece was designed using CAD for an exhibition at the National Galleries of Scotland and this fed into more experimentation with alternative approaches and new materials throughout the collections.

'I do a lot of bespoke work, making hats for clients going to special events, the racing, weddings, investitures, etc. It's lovely to meet new people and help them to look and feel fabulous. I meet a diversity of ladies from all walks of life, and for me it's about finding that balance of shape, colour and trim that brings out their personality and suits their outfit and colouring, whilst being appropriate for the occasion. You know when someone feels great in a hat – their body language changes; when a woman looks in the mirror and sees the finished hat with a huge smile on her face – that is a wonderful feeling!'

Sally-Ann's client base is testament to the wonder of her creations. Her hats have graced the heads of members of the Royal

Family, including the Princesses Beatrice and Eugenie, First Minister Nicola Sturgeon, mezzo soprano Katherine Jenkins, broadcaster and presenter Edith Bowman, ITV's Charlotte Hawkins, Channel 4's Gina Harding … the list is long and illustrious.

Each piece is designed and made with great attention to detail and finish. Sally-Ann is Scottish Opera's milliner, and other clients include the BBC, Scottish Ballet, the Royal Lyceum Theatre, and she also worked on the Robert de Niro film *The Good Shepherd* and the stage musical *The Lion King*. 'Because my work is so closely related to the wearer – having my hats worn by well-respected elegant women in the public eye such as members of the Royal Family, the First Minister, and internationally renowned performers is a validation for me that my work is of the highest quality. I feel proud and also privileged and humbled. When clients return to me for new hats or recommend me to their friends and family – that is a validation – a wonderful feeling.'

With so much time spent designing and creating alone in her workspace, Sally-Ann appreciates being part of Beaverhall Studios, where she's surrounded by other talented makers and designers working in a variety of disciplines. There's always time to meet other creatives and people running their own small businesses, offering an opportunity to spark exciting ideas and new directions.

Food for the milliner's soul comes from the peaceful zone of tranquillity that is the Royal Botanic Gardens – a place to walk and let the mind wander, when your mind is free of the concerns of the day, allowing the ideas to start to flow. 'We are all constantly surrounded by imagery – both natural and created, we soak it in and process it. Sometimes an experience, or the most insignificant of things, can inspire a seed of an idea, days or even years later.'

Sally-Ann relishes visits to the Fashion and Applied Arts collection at the National Museum of Scotland – and she has the honour of being featured in their Fashion and Style Gallery. The V&A Dundee have named her as one of their 'Design Champions' and she has shown nationally and internationally – including London Fashion Week, Origin, 'Dressed to Kilt' in New York, and 'UK Now' in Australia.

There's a new diffusion range under way for men and women – a collection of wool felt and casual straw hats including the most striking fedoras and trilbies, all ready to wear and all beautifully handcrafted. Running any business is a challenge and a creative one can be even more so, but this talented designer has carved out a wonderful niche in millinery and will no doubt be turning heads for a long time to come.

www.sallyannprovan.co.uk
www.facebook.com/SallyAnnProvanMillinery
Instagram: @sallyannhats
Twitter: @sallyannprovan

Mette Fruergaard-Jensen

MAKER – WOOD AND METAL

After working for twenty-five years as a potter, Danish maker Mette Fruergaard-Jensen started to work in wood and metals in an exciting new direction.

With both her parents working as potters, it seemed inevitable that Mette might also work in some form of craft. She was taken to the Copenhagen Co-operative Shop 'Den Petmanente' as a child, where her father was a member, and recalls, at 8 years old, how interested she was in it, so much so she even remembers the artists' names and their work from some of these early visits. 'I was so inspired, it has stayed with me all this time. And the forms I saw, the ones I liked I still remember, and they continue to inform my work today.'

A graduate in the 1960s of the Copenhagen Art and Craft School, now known as the Danish Design School, Mette forged a career working with earthenware and stoneware. But then she stopped, having lost interest in that discipline and thinking it was over and done with. She even thought she might leave craft altogether. 'But when you work in craft, you think about it all the time. You think of the problems and how to solve them. And I missed that.' Mette then took some weekend courses in jewellery and woodworking. However, it was when she did a workshop to create a Shaker-type box, using a steam-bending process, that she was hooked once again by the love of making, and feeling blessed that she'd found this opportunity to work in a completely different discipline. Mette realised that, of course, it didn't have to be wood but could be other materials, too, and started using the metals that now seem like a signature of her innovative and

original work. Having worked so long as a potter, she also found she could extrapolate all the knowledge and experience she already had in living and working as a maker to this new discipline.

Mette moved to Edinburgh eighteen years ago and realised that she hadn't lived in a city for twenty-two years. But she fell in love with Edinburgh and all its cultural life. Now she smilingly says, 'I'll die here, never leave it, it was such a good change for me.'

Mette now creates exquisitely crafted lidded boxes in a variety of materials. Different kinds of hardwood are used, mostly elm, beech and mahogany, and sometimes bog oak, ebony or burr elm. The metals she works with are aluminium, copper and brass. The boxes are quite architectural and the blend of organic and industrial is reflective of her Danish background. The craftsmanship is so precise, the materials all cut and sanded to fit so perfectly together that it's hard to resist touching them – running your hand along the different textures used in each piece, enjoying the smoothness of the wood, the change in feel of the metals and resins; it's a delightful experience combining the touch with the visual observations. We can see the natural beauty in the materials themselves and we're also awed by the artisanship involved in the making process.

Mette has schooled herself in how to use the range of tools and materials needed for her designs. When finding resin frames in second-hand shops to use in her practice became difficult because they'd gone out of fashion, Mette taught herself to make her own resin moulds and sheets. She is continuously on the lookout for new materials to absorb into her practice. Mette nearly always creates boxes, and now would rarely make a bowl. For her, it needs to be a closed shape and she sees her work not as sculpture but as something functional – although she's not creating things for any specific use. It's up to the buyer to give the form purpose. 'Putting materials together is a big thing for me, what kind of metal with what kind of wood. Materials are as important as working with form, proportion, surface, colour and texture.'

Her studio space is full of all the materials she's interested in and also strewn with the inventive work that she creates. The walls are covered in images that outline her process and give an indication of how diverse the materials, sizes and shapes can be. Samples of wood and metal are also on the walls, with colour swatches and samples of the resin sheets she's created. Pieces of beautiful wood with wonderful textures are filed against each other, waiting to be chosen and used.

The jewellery courses Mette did when she gave up pottery stood her in good stead too, having gained the knowledge of how to solder and work with metal. By heating the copper, she learned that the colours can be manipulated whilst patterns can be laid into the metallic surfaces.

The work is also about the contrasts in the material and how the properties of each work in tandem with each other, making them fit and mould together.

The wood and metals are sourced from local merchants. In the past it had been possible to visit scrapyards and find copper sheets, for instance, to recycle, but they're no longer open to the public and roadside skips, once a great source for the artist forager, are seen less and less. Occasionally a little gem might be found, a small Mahogany coffee table for instance, that she will liberate from a landfill future. The wood used must be seasoned, as older wood is easier to cut and manipulate. Offcuts from local furniture makers are a precious resource too. 'I start with an idea or a drawing of the box I want to make, but it changes during the process. I may add other elements or use other techniques than I first thought. I enjoy the process and the silent language of materials.'

The process involves using a bandsaw, metal cutter and blowtorch, and sometimes the way the wood is cut initially can inspire the shape the box will take. A personal sanding tool has been specially created using steel wool which gives a particularly frosted finish that Mette likes for some of the metals. The machinery can be a time saver in what is already a demanding process but the work is most enjoyable when solving problems along the way. It starts with a quick sketch and then the materials are gathered together to create what's in her imagination. Next it's working out how everything will fit together. The process is quite traditional and Mette has gained her experience just by working with the materials, learning how they can be shaped and worked to lie comfortably side by side. She's also a fan of YouTube, where you can always find films and tutorials on various technical processes – patination on metal, for example – that are helpful when working on new projects, or learning how to actually manoeuvre and physically handle the materials in the right way. Hard woods are a favourite to work with but occasionally soft woods are used and it was the cutting of pine into 5cm pieces that inspired a series of stunning candlesticks that were then teamed with resin, black stoneware and aluminium.

But it's the beautiful boxes that Mette is best known for, and she exhibits in Edinburgh and other places in the UK, as well as back in Denmark. 'I have had my studio in Coburg House for nine years. It's a space to work and also a space to present my work at Open Studios with information and images on the wall showing my work processes. I get great pleasure in people's reactions to my work and listening to their remarks. They often say they haven't seen anything like it.'

The work is very much admired and customers tend to come back and buy more pieces, creating their own Fruergaard-Jensen collection at home.

'I get great pleasure in people's reactions to my work and listening to their remarks. They often say they haven't seen anything like it.'

Mette really appreciates her space in the studio complex, enjoying and taking inspiration from the proximity of other artists, and the feeling of community – the sharing of information, of learning about exhibitions and galleries. 'If I had a studio on my own I would really miss this.' Inspiration is also found in visits to the Art and Design Department of the Central Library in Edinburgh where their treasure trove of books on different art processes and disciplines informs new work, covering almost everything Mette might need to know in her research. She finds the process of learning new techniques in the quiet of the library peaceful and insightful.

'I'm grateful that I have worked for fifty years now with something that interests me so much. Now that I'm old I have much more freedom and love living and working here.'

And it isn't just Edinburgh but the whole of Scotland that appeals so strongly to Mette. The Danish population is roughly the same size as Scotland but only half the area and the very flat landscape is generally covered in agriculture. Mette loves the contrast she has found in the landscape here, especially in the Hebrides, and she spends time walking on Harris and Lewis, Mull, Iona and Isla, to name just a few, with a particular favourite being Barra. 'Islands are good for walking because you always know where you are.' She loves the rolling hills, the rich textures and amazing colour palette she finds there and it's an enjoyable contrast to the city.

Mette has exhibited in many places in the UK and internationally, including the Open Eye Gallery Edinburgh, Visual Arts Scotland, Danish Diaspora Exhibition and SOFA Chicago.

www.mettefruergaardjensen.com
www.facebook.com/mettefruergaardjensen
Instagram: @mettefruergaardjensenboxes

Image Credits

All images in the book belong to the author with the exception of those listed below:

Alistair Clark
Pages 9, 12, 16, 52–3, 55, 57–8, 60–2, 96, 112, 114, 131–3, 134, 144–5, 146, 172, 174–6

Andrea Thomson
Page 38, 158

Craft Design House
Page 130

David Stanton
Page 25

Elizabeth Jane Campbell
Pages 45–8

Ellie Morag
Page 151, 154

Emily Hogarth
Page 41–2,

Hannah Louise Lamb
Pages 126–7

Judy R. Clark
Page 26

Julien Borghino
Pages 165, 167–9

Further Information

If you've been inspired by what you've read and seen in this book, you may want to know more. Below are listed organisations that run studios and workspaces that you can contact to find out about vacant spaces, or open weekends. Also listed are places to go in Edinburgh to see and buy craft produced by skilled artists and makers, whether they are permanent shops or annual exhibitions that you might want to visit. Details of the wonderful photographers used in the book are also set out below.

Studios in Edinburgh

Albion Road Studios
78 Albion Road
Edinburgh EH7 5QZ
www.waspsstudios.org.uk

Beaverhall Art Studios
27 Beaverhall Road
Edinburgh EH7 4JE

Coburg House Studios
15 Coburg Street
Edinburgh EH6 6ET
www.coburghouse.co.uk

Creative Showroom
336C Leith Walk, Edinburgh EH6 5BR
www.thecreativeshowroom.com

Out of the Blue Drill Hall
36 Dalmeny Street Edinburgh EH6 8RJ
www.outoftheblue.org.uk

Patriot Hall
Wasps Scotland Ltd
Edinburgh EH3 5AY
www.waspsstudios.org.uk

Abbeymount Studios
2 Easter Road EH7 5AN
www.ootbabbeymountstudios.org.uk

St Margaret's House
151 London Road
Edinburgh EH7 6AE
www.edinburghpalette.co.uk

West Park Place
Wasps Scotland
2–3 West Park Place
Dalry Road
Edinburgh EH11 2DP
www.waspsstudios.org.uk

Where to buy Scottish craft in Edinburgh

Coburg Studios Gallery Shop
15 Coburg Street
Edinburgh EH6 6ET

Concrete Wardrobe
50A Broughton Street
Edinburgh EH1 3SA

Cranachan & Crowdie
263 Canongate
Edinburgh EH8 8BQ

Curiouser & Curiouser
93 Broughton Street
Edinburgh EH1 3RZ

Scottish Design Exchange
Ocean Terminal
Edinburgh EH6 6JJ

The Adam Pottery
76 Henderson Row
Edinburgh EH3 5BJ

The Red Door Gallery
42 Victoria Street
Edinburgh EH1 2JW

The Scottish Gallery
16 Dundas Street
Edinburgh EH3 6HZ

Craft Scotland Summer Show – every August
2nd Floor at White Stuff
George Street
Edinburgh EH2 3ES

The National Museum of Scotland
Chambers Street
Edinburgh EH1 1JF

Useful organisations and exhibitions

Applied Arts Scotland
www.appliedartsscotland.org.uk

Craft Scotland
www.craftscotland.org

Creative Scotland
www.creativescotland.com

Dazzle
www.dazzle-exhibitions.co.uk

Design Exhibition Scotland
www.designexhibitionscotland.co.uk

Elements
www.elementsfestival.co.uk

Goldsmiths' Fair
www.goldsmithsfair.co.uk

Handmade Britain
www.handmadeinbritain.co.uk

London Design Fair
www.londondesignfair.co.uk

MADE London
www.madelondon-marleybone.co.uk

UK Crafts Council
www.craftscouncil.org.uk

Photographers

Alistair Clark: www.alistairclarkphotography.co.uk
Andrea Thomson: www.andreathomsonphotography.com
David Stanton: www.stantonimaging.co.uk
Ellie Morag: www.elliemorag.com
Julien Borghino: www.julienborghino.com
Leonard Rankin
Linda Jones: www.facebook.com/greenshoots.photog
Marc Millar: www.marcmillarphotography.co.uk
Martin Alan Smith: www.martinalansmith.com
Nancy MacDonald: nancymacdonald.co.uk
Niall McTaggart: www.niallmactaggartphotography.co.uk
Paul Cowan: www.paultcowan.com
Paul Hartley: www.hartleystudios.com
Rachel Hein: www.rachelhein.com
Shannon Tofts: www.shannontofts.com
Stuart McClay: www.stuartmcclay.com
Susan Castillo: www.susancastillo.co.uk
Suzanne Heffron: www.suzanneheffron.com

Written by
Eddie Rowley and Katherine Rogers

Designed by Joanna Davies

Published by Grandreams Limited
435-437 Edgware Road, Little Venice, London W2 1TH

contents

Ronan

Personally Speaking

How have you coped with the loss of your dear mother, Marie?

As you can imagine, it's been traumatic for me and all the family. She was the rock in our life. She was my best friend. I miss her. I miss her like mad. I'd give up all the success with Boyzone to have her back.

Do you enjoy being famous?

Well, first of all, fame is not a word that I associate with myself. I'm just Ro, an ordinary person like everyone else. The only difference is, lots of people know me because I'm an entertainer.

How did you end up in show business?

It's what I always wanted to do, really. I wanted to be in the public eye. It could have been sports but in the end it turned out to be entertainment.

What kind of sport did you consider?

Well, I was a good athlete and I always thought I'd end up representing my country as a runner. I was offered a scholarship to an American college to do track, but then the band came along.

What have been your biggest thrills?

Oh, God, there have been lots. I've been so lucky in the business. I got to host the Eurovision Song Contest. And presenting the MTV awards was a real buzz. It was an adrenaline rush and I felt pretty cool and important. But then it's on to the next thing.

What do you love about performing?

I love watching the kids smiling when we're on stage performing. Watching them singing the songs back and the happiness that brings. I love that. It's a very special feeling. A feeling that we do make a difference to their lives in a good way.

Now that you've grown into a man, do you ever think about changing the name of Boyzone?

Yeah, we've thought about it. Obviously it doesn't reflect the people we are now because we are a lot older. But it's only a name and not an image. We do like it being abbreviated to BZ. A lot of people call us BZ now, which is cool.

Are you comfortable with the fact that you've matured?

Yeah, it is good to have a sense of knowing what you're doing and what you're about. When we started out we were really green and naive and we had to rely on other people to find a path for us. Now we have the experience so we take full control of what we do.

Do you still get star struck?

Absolutely. I never get used to meeting people who are legends in the business. When you bump into stars like Elton John or George Michael I'm definitely in awe of them. They're like the royalty of the music business.

Are you comfortable with being a sex symbol?

Me, a sex symbol? No way, man. I don't see myself as a sex symbol and I certainly don't portray myself as one. It's the media that does that. I'm fashion conscious and I love clothes, but I don't spend time looking in the mirror and grooming myself. And I don't have an all-year-round tan, in fact I don't have a tan at all.

Do girls send you naughty items of clothing in the post?

Sadly, no, not that I'd encourage it. So what do I get? Well, ever since I revealed that I wear a sticky plaster on my finger for good luck, fans have been sending me sack loads of them. I don't think I'll have to buy a box of plasters again.

Are you glad you got married?

Absolutely, Yvonne has made me so happy. I'd had a terrible year after my mam's death and Yvonne was my rock. She helped me through it. Our relationship is based on friendship and love. When we married in the Caribbean it was the greatest moment of my life. I'm just so happy.

Some people are afraid to talk about religion, but you have no problems in that regard?

Well, I don't preach about my beliefs. If I'm asked in interviews, I'll tell journalists that my faith is important. I'm not ashamed to say I love the Lord.

What will you do after Boyzone?

I don't want to think that far ahead. I love Boyzone. I love every minute of it. I'll be lost when it's over. I just don't want to think about it.

boyz on Ronan

Keith: I love Ronan an awful lot. I'm very close to him. He is a very good ambassador. I am not jealous and don't resent him in any way. He deserves everything he has.

Steve: He's a great friend to have. Ronan is very thoughtful and caring. He cares about everyone. And he looks after all of us. He's very sensitive to everyone's needs. He's like a big brother, even though he's the youngest member of Boyzone.

Mikey: Ronan has fantastic qualities as a person. He puts everyone else before himself. There isn't a selfish bone in his body.

Shane: He's a great organiser. He's always on top of everything. Ronan takes on a huge workload and seems to thrive on being under pressure. He's a tremendously talented pop performer and a top bloke.

boyz on Steve

Ronan: Stevo is a very shy, sensitive guy. We get on very well. We're always having a laugh. I think he's a very creative guy and he'll do well after Boyzone, probably as an actor.

Shane: He can be very funny at times. He makes me laugh when we're together. He's a good guy to have around. He's always on the telephone.

Keith: He's a pretty cool bloke in my eyes. You couldn't say a bad word about Steve. He's just a good guy.

Mikey: When we started out, Steve was very shy and very homesick. Now he has grown up with Boyzone and I think he has gained a lot more confidence.

boyz on Mikey

Ronan: Sometimes he can be very serious, but he's also a good laugh. He's a bit of a contradiction in that respect. He loves being up on stage and always enjoys a performance.

Steve: He can be pretty deep at times and he's got a strong personality. He knows what he wants and where he's going. I think he's a lucky guy in that respect.

Keith: Mikey enjoys a laugh and I like that in a guy. If you were ever in trouble, Mikey would always be there for you. He's very loyal.

Shane: I think he worries a lot. He's often deep in thought. But he's very genuine and you always know where you stand with him. He's a good bloke.

boyz on Keith

Ronan: He's very honest. He speaks his mind and you always know where you stand with Keith. There's no hidden agenda. He's a fun guy to be around.

Steve: He's like a big brother to me. He's very considerate. People think that he's flippant about life, but he has a serious side to him. If you're feeling down, he'll have a reassuring word. He's a guy you can discuss your problems with.

Mikey: Keith and I are very alike in some respects and, consequently, we sometimes rub each other up the wrong way. He knows how to wind people up, but he never pushes it too far. And I have to say, there isn't a bad bone in his body.

Shane: We've always been good mates. Keith used to go out with me sister, so needless to say, I think he's a good bloke. He's very funny and always game for a laugh.

boyz on Shane

Ronan: He's the Mr Cool of Boyzone. Shano is very laid back. Nothing ruffles him. I envy that side of his nature. He'll live to be a very old man because he won't let things get him down.

Keith: He's a guy who enjoys life. He doesn't take himself too seriously. We've been friends since we were kids and that's something that'll never change.

Mikey: He's a poser, he'll tell you that himself. But he's not at all big headed. And he's a great guy to have for a friend. Shane will always listen to your troubles and give you good advice.

Steve: He's very kind and considerate. He'll always look out for you. If you're feeling down, Shane will try his best to perk you up. I think he's a great guy.

five on five

fact file

Keith

KEITH DUFFY

PLACE OF BIRTH: DUBLIN

DATE OF BIRTH: 1.10.74

STAR SIGN: LIBRA

HEIGHT: 6' 1"

STATUS: A DAD - HIS LITTLE SON IS CALLED JORDAN

FAVOURITE FORM OF RELAXATION: WORKING OUT IN A GYM

FAVOURITE SPORT: MOTOR RACING

AMBITION: TO WORK ON TV AFTER BOYZONE

homezone

Mikey

If you really want to know someone, you have to live with them. So who knows Mikey better than his family? Mikey has just one brother and five sisters, including twins Claire and Debbie. He's the baby in the family. Claire spills the beanz on her little brother.

What was it like in your home growing up with Mikey?
Well, boys are boys, and they tend to be loud around the house. Mikey was a bit like that, but we always got on well because he was close to us in age and he was the youngest boy. Niall is a lot older than him. Like every normal family we had our rows, but there was also a lot of fun in the house with Mikey around. And even though he was the baby, he never got any special treatment.

Can you remember his first day at school?
I remember there was a lot of trauma in the house because Mikey created a dreadful scene. He just didn't want to go. He was kicking and screaming and eventually Mam had to tie him down and bring him in a pram.

Is he a mammy's boy or a daddy's boy?
Like all Irish boys, he's a mammy's boy. Mikey and Mum are very close. They get on really well and have chats together that go on for ages.

Was he a telltale?
Not that I remember. I don't recall him getting any of us into trouble with our parents.

What are your earliest memories of Mikey?
He was always messing around with radios and motors. He was a typical boy like that. Always pulling things apart and trying to make something out of them. Later, when he became a mechanic I wasn't surprised. He was very good at things like that.

Did he ever show any signs that he might be famous one day?
Oh yeah, he was always very keen on being in the limelight. When he was very young he went to drama school and was one of the few boys there. And as a kid he appeared in an advert for Mikado biscuits.

Did he get any encouragement from the family to join Boyzone?
Well, Dad in particular was behind him from the very start. He encouraged Mikey to go for the auditions. We were all very supportive and were thrilled when he got into Boyzone.

What were Mikey's big interests when he was a teenager?
Oh, definitely cars. Like most boys, he was car mad. He still is. He was thrilled when he got his first car at 17. He was always stuck under the bonnet checking out the engine.

Do you think Mikey is really happy?
I don't think he could be any happier. Life has been very good to him. He's had a brilliant career with Boyzone, travelled around the world and seen amazing places. And he's a proud dad. He's absolutely cracked about little Hannah.

On the Road

Boyzone like to party when they're on the road, touring and promoting their albums. It helps to cope with the pressures of stardom and the non-stop work regime that comes with success.

Ronan says: "We're not bad Boyz, but at the same time we're not as squeaky clean as the media sometimes present us. We do like to party till late. But hey, that's not a bad thing, is it?"

Keith used to be the wildest of the bunch, but he's toned down his social activities in the last year. Getting a bar bill of a whopping £6,000 at the end of one tour was a bit of a shocker for him. "I was the life and soul of the party every night, buying drinks for everyone. I couldn't believe it when I got the bill," he says.

But although they admit to being wild Boyz now and then, Boyzone don't tarnish their clean-cut image. None of the Fab Five smokes or does drugs. They are all vehemently opposed to the use of drugs and their advice to young people is to steer clear of them.

Steve admits: "There are drugs in the community where I come from in Dublin and I have seen them destroy the lives of people I knew. It's so sad. Drugs wreck your life, so stay away from them. They're not cool."

Ronan says: "Getting up on stage and performing is better than any drug".

Before shows there are often several hours to kill and the Boyz pass the time doing different things. Shane can often be found on his BMX bike, skates or rollerblades backstage. Keith and Mikey often play basketball with the Boyzone crew. Ronan is usually busy doing interviews and Steve listens to music or just enjoys a quiet time with his own thoughts. Keith will run around entertaining all and sundry with his jokes, which are often so silly but they still make you laugh.

Just before they're due on stage, Ro usually knocks back a hot lemon and honey drink to keep his voice in top condition. Steve will be gossiping in corridors with passers-by. Shane can be usually found doing his stretching exercises. Keith refuses to relax and is usually causing mayhem. Mikey sits quietly in a corner with his guitar or Nintendo game.

After shows, it's back to their hotel and the Boyz will wind down by having a couple of drinks and a sing-song in the residents' lounge. Mikey is usually the first to start a song...he's got an extensive range of golden oldie hits from yesteryear that probably only your mums and dads will know. Shane rarely participates in after-show events. He's not big into drinking and is usually the first to retire to bed to catch up on his sleep.

Shane

Personally Speaking

Do you feel you're getting old?
Well, I suppose we're all getting old. That's just nature taking its course. I suppose I'm slowing down and getting a bit sore in my bones. It's only natural. But I'm not finished yet. There's a lot more life left in this boy. I'm mad for life and living.

Can you not handle partying every night?
No (laughs). I can't do it anymore. I'm an old man. I can only handle one late night a week. I sit at home and knit.

Have you got any bad habits?
Well, I tend to belch a lot. I know people think it's rude, but I don't get embarrassed because I feel it's a natural thing to do. It's just getting up wind. It could be worse.

Why do you always look so serious in photographs?
I get embarrassed if I'm asked to smile in photos. There's no point in asking me to look like I'm having a laugh, 'cos I don't do that. It doesn't mean I'm a very serious bloke. I really do enjoy life.

Is there any new skill you would like to master?
I'd love to be really good at martial arts. I'd love to go to somewhere like Japan and study it with the masters. Unfortunately I just don't have the time right now. Maybe some day.

Are you a romantic type of guy?
Yeah, in me own way. I do send flowers all the time. That's romantic, isn't it?

You're not one of the drinkers in the group?
Nah. I'll have a couple but I don't go mad. I got really sick from alcohol when I was young and it taught me a lesson. Me and some mates drank beer and Malibu when we were kids on holiday with my parents. We drank several pints in the space of 20 minutes – racing we were – and

I ended up being disgustingly sick. I couldn't move and had to be dragged home. I haven't been drunk since.

You've probably got the most distinctive image in the band. Do you get bored being asked about it all the time?
No way. I put a lot of work into it so it's great that people recognise that I make the effort. It's the feature that makes me stand out in the group.

You give the impression that you're not approachable. Is that a true reflection of your personality?
Nah, not at all. Because of the way I look, people think I'm aggressive. But nothing could be further from the truth. It's just that I'm quite reserved and I only speak whenever I have to speak. I don't blabber on all the time. I'm a nice person if I want to know somebody.

Do you feel that Boyzone is burning you out?
No way, man. Boyzone gives me life. Being in this group keeps me motivated. There's always something new and interesting to do, so it's my engine.

You get thousands of letters from fans. Do you get a chance to read any of them?
Yeah, I read as much as I can. Obviously I don't read them all. I don't like reading. But I'll read short letters, so keep them brief.

What kind of things make you angry?
I'm not the sort of bloke who gets angry. I'm a lucky guy because I'm very laid back. My attitude is, whatever happens, happens. I don't get stressed out over things. I'll have me say but I don't lose me head.

Will you still be shaving your eyebrow when you're an old geezer?
Yeah. It's me image. I'm stuck with it now.

fact file

Steve

STEPHEN GATELY

PLACE OF BIRTH: DUBLIN

DATE OF BIRTH: 17.3.76

STAR SIGN: PISCES

HEIGHT: 5' 7"

COLOUR OF EYES: BLUE

FAVOURITE FOOD:
CAJUN CHICKEN

FAVOURITE MOVIES:
ALL THE DISNEY FILMS

FAVOURITE POSSESSION:
HIS NEW CAR

On the R

ecord

Ronan

• When I went to a new school in the country some of the boys didn't like me 'cos I was from Dublin. They ganged up on me, but I sorted them out. That was my first big fight.

• I remember getting my first wage packet when I was 15 and working in a shoe shop.

• When I was young I was the only one in the family who came back from the shops with the right things. I was such a goody goody.

• Come to Ireland for a holiday because it's the most beautiful country in the world and we live there.

• It means an awful lot to us to think that our fans care so much.

• I was 17 when I got my first car. It was a white banger and it cost me £400.

• As a kid I stole some sweets from our local shop, but I ate the evidence.

• When I was young I couldn't save a penny – money used to burn a hole in my pocket.

• I don't regret anything I did. I'm here today because I did what I did. I don't regret any of it.

Steve

- At school, a teacher wouldn't let me go to the toilet one day so I sat there and did it in me trousers.

- In school, I always tried to stick up for everyone that was bullied.

- The Boyzone auditions were nerve-racking. I remember seeing all these blokes there and thinking, I haven't a chance in the world.

- My house is haunted. My brother Alan came in the bedroom one night and asked, 'Have you got a light?' and the lighter just flew off the wardrobe.

- You can see me for a split second in the movie, *The Commitments*. There's a market scene at the start where me and me mam are haggling.

- If I can be like a kid all the time, then I will.

- My mum still tells me off about going to bed early, taking my vitamins, sitting down and relaxing more often, especially when I'm at home.

Shane

- I once got caught mitching (bunking) off school. I went to a shopping centre with a mate but he ratted on me, so he wasn't a friend anymore.

- My father respected my decision to leave school early to work as a mechanic because he knew I hated it.

- I used to look at New Kids On The Block posters when I was about 11 and say to myself that someday I'd be like them.

- I like me clothes. I just try to wear things that look a bit different from the rest of the band.

- I think Will Smith is the coolest guy on the planet.

- I'd like to have four kids.

Keith

- I was once suspended from primary school for letting off three stink-bombs. The stink was unbelievable.

- I once got a bad head injury when I was playing the Irish game of hurling and ended up in hospital for three weeks.

- When I was young I threw a rock at a bloke on the road I was fighting with, but it missed and smashed my mother's windscreen.

- I went out with Shane's sister Alison when I was 15. She asked me out and we were together for about three or four weeks.

- The first time I felt like I had to be a grown up was when Jordan was born.

- I went to see *The Full Monty* and I wet myself laughing. I really fell out of the place laughing.

- I got told off by my mother for cursing in front of little Jordan.

Mikey

• My mum, Sheila, and myself are very close. We send cards to each other addressed to 'my pal'.

• I didn't like my first teacher at school. She used to grab me by the ears when I was disruptive in class.

• I don't think I'm famous. I never see it that way.

• Sometimes I look to the future and think, 'Will I ever be grown up?'

• I only lie if I have to...and only if it's a very small one.

• I have many, many regrets.

• I used to get very homesick, but now England feels like home to me.

Ronan

RONAN KEATING

PLACE OF BIRTH: DUBLIN

DATE OF BIRTH: 3.3.77

STAR SIGN: PISCES

HEIGHT: 5' 9"

COLOUR OF EYES: BLUE

STATUS: MARRIED (TO YVONNE)

FAVOURITE FOOD:
A CURRY DISH HIS
LATE MOTHER USED TO MAKE

FAVOURITE ARTISTS:
GEORGE MICHAEL,
R KELLY, BRIAN KENNEDY

Mikey

Personally Speaking

What is the best thing that's happened to you in your life?

Apart from Boyzone, it's the unbelievable love that my little daughter Hannah has brought into my life. Words can't adequately express the feelings I have for Hannah. She's just absolutely fantastic and gorgeous and I couldn't imagine life without her.

Do you ever get really emotional and break down?

Not really. It's actually something I regret because they say a good cry now and then is good for you. It's a release valve when things build up. Sometimes I get upset over the fact that I'm away from my little daughter for long periods when Boyzone travel around the world. That can be difficult to deal with. But it has to be done.

What's the worst thing about being in Boyzone?

Apart from the long separations from Hannah, it's the early mornings. They're a real killer. Sometimes it feels like you're getting up in the middle of the night. That's the horrible part. Having to get out of bed and deal with the world when all you want to do is sleep.

Are you happy in Boyzone?

Yeah, especially now that the music has matured. I was a bit unsure about it all at the beginning because I'm older than the other lads and I was into different music. Sting, Eric Clapton and Bob Dylan are among my favourites. It was hard for me, but now I'm very comfortable with the music and songs of Boyzone. I love this band.

What's the best thing about being in Boyzone?

I think it's definitely the fact that I've made four good friends who're going to be there for me for the rest of my life as I will be for them. We're 'brothers in arms'. We've experienced so much together. Nobody can ever take that away from us. We'll always be friends, no matter what.

How have you handled fame?

I feel I've got to grips with it pretty well, all things considered. It's a strange thing, fame. Being recognised wherever you go. People you've never met knowing your name, knowing things about you. But it's been a gradual thing and I've got used to it. Now if people weren't paying attention I'd be worried because there'd be something wrong.

Has your life in Boyzone got easier or more difficult in the last few years?

A bit of both, really. It's certainly busier because of the huge level of success we've enjoyed. But we're also a lot more experienced now so it's easier to deal with whatever comes your way. It's more enjoyable now, definitely.

Are you a clean-living band?

Well, that depends on what you mean about clean living. We try to be good role models for young people in that we're opposed to drugs and that kind of thing. But we go out and have a good time, have a couple of drinks and go clubbing. Not a lot, but certainly now and then. We want to enjoy life. We're not boring characters.

What has been the most expensive treat you've allowed yourself since Boyzone's success?

I suppose me house. I don't know if you'd call that a treat, it's more of a necessity. But it's certainly my biggest expense.

What kind of life will you have after Boyzone?

Well, I hope I will still have a career in the music business. I'd love to do a solo album and perform my own music and songs in live shows. That's my ambition. That's my dream. Time will tell, but it's what I'm going to pursue after Boyzone.

Which of the Boyz in the band are you most like?

Keith, definitely. Me and Keith, we're the same kind of animal. We're so alike in many ways. We've got strong personalities. We often rub each other up the wrong way as a result. We tend to spark off each other now and then, but we never let things get out of control.

What's the worst feature of Mikey Graham's personality?

I suppose it's the fact that I'm a worrier. I get very serious about things, they play on my mind and I have to work them out. But I get there in the end.

Ronan, Steve, Keith, Mikey and Shane may be our dreams come true, but what do the Boyz yearn for?

DREAM

zone

DREAM house

Keith: I'd love an estate like the computer billionaire Bill Gates. It's huge and full of gadgets and gimmicks. The whole place is run by computers and computer technology – the windows, the doors, the gates, the temperature – everything's connected to computers. You could sit in bed and control everything.

Mikey: I'd love a house with its own lake or river or on the coast. I love water around me – it's very relaxing and soothing. I've always thought owning your own lake would be great. I'd swim in it, fish in it, and it'd be all mine.

Steve: I'd like a cottage way out in the remotest countryside miles away from everywhere. I'd love an old windswept stone cottage on some land in the wilds of nowhere. I grew up in the inner city and I've always dreamed I'd love to live in the country. That said, I'd probably go mad in a few days and run back to town.

Ronan: I think I already have my dream house. It's in the country but it's only a half an hour from the city and it's big enough for all my family to enjoy and to have friends stay over. The only thing I'd like outside of that might be a small holiday home abroad.

Shane: I'd love a penthouse apartment in Manhattan. I think New York's a real exciting place to live and I'd love to live in the heart of it. I'd like a really modern apartment all chrome, steel and glass overlooking the city.

DREAM car

Mikey: It has to be a Dodge Viper V10 Engine. These two-seaters are called 'American Muscle'. It's a mad car, you'd certainly be noticed in it.

Ronan: The Aston Martin DB6 convertible is handmade in Britain. It's everyone's dream car – real James Bond with all the gimmicks. I think Prince Charles has one hasn't he?

Keith: I'd love a Lamborghini Diablo. It's a 12 cylinder two-seater which can do 200mph and I love the black smoke windows.

Steve: I did a television advert with the national lottery and there was a vintage Ferrari Dino in it that was an absolute beauty. I'd love that.

Shane: I want to drive a Jordan Formula One car in Formula One racing. If I can't do that I'll have a Ferrari F50. It's a Formula One car that's road legal.

DREAM holiday

Shane: My dream holiday would be in the pit row of a Formula One race anywhere in the world. But I'd really love to be in Monza for the San Marino Grand Prix. I've never had the time off to be there before but I'll get there yet.

Steve: I've already had a dream holiday in the Caribbean that I'd love to repeat. There's no place as dreamy and romantic in the world than watching a sunset in Antigua. It's a real taste of paradise.

Keith: My dream holiday would be to travel across the United States for a few months. I'd love to drive right across the US from New York to California in a fast convertible and no-limit credit cards. I want to see all the States of America. Each one of them is like a different country.

Mikey: I'd like to learn how to scuba dive and go diving in some of the best coral reefs in the world. I've seen documentaries about diving and I've always said if I had the time I'll do a basic training course and spend a few weeks diving in a place like Thailand or

Australia. It always looks so peaceful and so beautiful. Well, it does on the telly anyway.

Ronan: We went touring in South America last year and we were all bowled over by the countries there. I'd love to go back for a few months and really get to know places like Mexico, Chile and Argentina. South America has absolutely everything from fabulous cities like Buenos Aires to totally untamed jungles. Visiting South America was a real eye opener for me.

DREAM ambition

Shane: That's easy – I want to race cars. I want to be a Formula One driver in the Monte Carlo or San Marino Grand Prix. I wonder would Eddie Jordan give me a job after Boyzone?

Steve: I'd love to write or perform a soundtrack to a Disney movie. I've had part of the dream come true when I sang a track on *Hercules*. But I'd love to work on an entire soundtrack.

Mikey: I'd like to get into more rock-orientated music after Boyzone. That's basically the style of music that I like personally. I'd like to write or perform my own music. That would be a dream for me I suppose.

Ronan: I hope that I'll always be in the music business. I don't really care what I do as long as I can stay in it. I wouldn't mind becoming a music presenter either. But I'd love to become a really successful songwriter. I'd love to write

songs that would become classics and that people would always remember.

Keith: I'd just like to be as happy for the rest of my life as I am now. I'm doing something that I love right now. I hope I'll always be able to do something that I love and that I'll always be able to provide and look after my family.

DREAM woman

Ronan: My ideal woman would be a combination of Dawn French and Gwyneth Paltrow. I love the company of women who make me laugh and I love the classically simple looks of someone like Gwyneth Paltrow. I've never met Gwyneth but I've met Dawn French and she's absolutely brilliant.

Shane: I've already met my dream woman. Well, I have to say that or she'd kill me, wouldn't she?

Keith: I think Goldie Hawn would be my idea of an ideal woman. She's flirty, funny, smart and even though she must be fifty she still looks fabulous. She's getting better looking as she gets older. Did you see her on Ruby Wax's show on TV? She was fab!

Steve: The actress Isabella Rossellini is one of the most perfect-looking women I've ever seen. She has dark short hair and huge eyes and never seems to wear any make-up but looks so beautiful. She seems to exude mystery too. She is kind of aloof which is always attractive.

Mikey: There are too many dream women out there to count. If you're looking for a well known woman I think Uma Thurman and Julia Roberts look very attractive. But if I was to meet them, then maybe they wouldn't be attractive anymore – because your dream woman is not just about looks, it's a whole package. She has to be funny and have the right chemistry. She has to be smart and kind. There's so many reasons why you fall for someone and looks are just one part of it.

homez⊙ne

Keith

If you really want to get to know someone, you have to live with them. So who knows Keith better than his family?

Keith has two brothers, Derek (25) and John (17). We talked to John, a choreographer and dancer with champion hip-hop group Altern 8. John spilled the beanz on his big Boyzone brother.

What was it like growing up with Keith?
We had our ups and downs like any other family. Sometimes we killed each other. Other times we got on great. In some ways Boyzone has brought us closer together because we appreciate the bit of time we spend together now.

Who shared a room with Keith?
I did.

Was he tidy?
He was very tidy. He used to freak with me in the room. On a Saturday when I was out, he'd spend all day cleaning up the bedroom. He used to ask my mother to make me keep the room clean. I never cleaned it. He always did it.

Is he a mammy's boy or a daddy's boy?
He's definitely always a mammy's boy. He's a big softy.

Was he a telltale?
No, I was the telltale. But anytime I threatened to tell on him, he always had something that he could hold over me.

What are your earliest memories of Keith?
I remember when we used to take the school bus together to primary school in Belgrove. He'd leave his bag on the bus and tell me to carry it into the school yard for him.

Did you have nicknames for him?
Keith had really bad acne when he was younger and we used to call him pizza face. He'll kill me for that. We also used to call him 'Smelly Feet Keith' because he had really smelly feet. He still does.

Did you ever think he'd be famous?
No, never. I remember him telling us his friend, Shane Lynch, had joined this band and I really wanted him to join it too. But in the beginning he said "no way". Then he came home one day and said he was joining it too. I don't think anyone thought they would make the big time, but they did!

What interests do you share?
My favourite instrument is the drums and it's Keith's too. We both share an interest in music, basketball, dance and choreography. And going out on the town and enjoying ourselves.

Which brother is he closest to?
You'd have to ask him that. I'd say there are some things he'd talk to Derek about and wouldn't say to me. And there are some things he'd feel he could tell me and wouldn't say to Derek.

fact file

Shane

SHANE LYNCH

PLACE OF BIRTH: DUBLIN

DATE OF BIRTH: 3.7.76

STAR SIGN: CANCER

HEIGHT: 6'

COLOUR OF EYES: BLUE

STATUS:
MARRIED
(TO EASTHER OF ETERNAL)

FAVOURITE HOLIDAY DESTINATION:
JAMAICA

AMBITION:
TO BE A
MOTOR RACING DRIVER

Your number is up

The Boyz are number one in their fans' eyes but according to the science of numerology - Ronan is 3, Steve is 7, Keith is 5 and Shane and Mikey are 6. What are we talking about?

For thousands of years, the ancient Greeks and Chinese used numbers to reveal people's personalities. Numerologists say everyone has a birth date number between one and nine. Each number represents particular strengths, weaknesses and character traits. By working out your own birth date number you can discover some valuable insights into your personality.

Let's see what we can learn about the Boyz from the wisdom of this ancient culture. By calculating your own birth date number, you can also learn what numerology has to say about yourself.

How To Work Out Your Own Birth Date Number:
To discover your birth date number, add together the digits in the day, the month and the year of your birth until you arrive at a single digit.

Here's how we worked out the Boyz' Birth Date Numbers:

Keith

Date of birth 01/10/1974
Day 0 + 1 = 1
Day + Month 1 + 1 + 0 = 2
Day + Month + year
2 + 1 + 9 + 7 + 4 = 23
Add the digits 2 + 3 = 5

Keith's Birth Date
Number is: **5**

Steve

Date of birth 17/03/1976
Day 1 + 7 = 8
Day + Month 8 + 0 + 3 = 11
Day + Month + year
11 + 1 + 9 + 7 + 6 = 34
Add the digits 3 + 4 = 7

Steve's Birth Date
Number is: **7**

Ronan

Date of birth 03/03/1977
Day 0 + 3 = 3
Day + Month 3 + 0 + 3 = 6
Day + Month + year
6 + 1 + 9 + 7 + 7 = 30
Add the digits 3 + 0 = 3

Ronan's Birth Date
Number is: **3**

Shane

Date of birth 03/07/1976
Day 0 + 3 = 3
Day + Month 3 + 0 + 7 = 10
Day + Month + year
10 + 1 + 9 + 7 + 6 = 33
Add the digits 3 + 3 = 6

Shane's Birth Date
Number is: **6**

Mikey

Date of birth 15/08/1972
Day 1 + 5 = 6
Day + Month 6 + 0 + 8 = 14
Day + Month + year
14 + 1 + 9 + 7 + 2 = 33
Add the digits 3 + 3 = 6

Mikey's Birth Date
Number is: **6**

THE No.1 PERSON

Strengths:
Number one people are usually extroverts who possess qualities of leadership, courage, creativity, energy and enthusiasm. They are often single-minded about setting and achieving goals. They crave success and the adoration that goes with it. They are also generous and enthusiastic people.

Weaknesses:
The downside is that they can be bossy, aggressive and uncooperative. They can also be fickle, boastful and even lazy.

Career Choices:
Number one people are natural leaders. They make good inventors, producers, designers, directors and explorers.

Lucky Colour: Red

Famous No.1's:
Sean Connery, Harrison Ford, Whitney Houston, Martin Luther King, Mikhail Gorbachev.

THE No.2 PERSON

Strengths:
Number two people are caring peacemakers. They are gentle, diplomatic and wise. They also tend to be patient, trustworthy, loyal and sensitive. In short they make very good friends.

Weaknesses:
Unfortunately they can be overly sensitive and gullible. They are a con man's dream. They can also be moody and indecisive. They can be so overly cautious that they get nothing done.

Career Choices:
Number two people make very good diplomats, social workers, counsellors, nurses, politicians and lawyers. They are also creative so they make good writers, artists and dancers.

Lucky Colour: Orange

Famous No.2's:
Madonna, Shirley Bassey, Diana Ross, Prince Charles, Bill Clinton, Ronald Reagan.

THE No.3 PERSON
Ronan Keating

Strengths:
Number three people like Ronan are pleasure loving, happy, generous and full of life. Number three is also the symbol of logic, intelligence and reason. They are often inspiring, optimistic and creative and are very caring.

Weaknesses:
They can be scatterbrained flirts. They can also be extravagant, impractical and fretful. Worse still number three people can have bad tempers and a tendency to cheat!

Career Choices:
These are the people who are best at creating. They make good writers, artists, comedians and musicians. Any work that makes people feel better such as the priesthood, singing, acting, dancing or painting appeals to number three people.

Lucky Colour: Yellow

Famous No.3's:
Ronan Keating, Jane Austen, Bill Cosby, Alfred Hitchcock.

THE No.4 PERSON

Strengths:
Number four is the symbol of determination and practicality. Number four people are practical, responsible, reliable and disciplined. They tend to be neat, efficient, helpful, focused and hardworking. They think logically and act with honesty and loyalty.

Weaknesses:
Number fours can be impatient, bossy and even violent. They resist change. Some fours can become dull and narrow-minded.

Career Choices:
Physical and mental building work suits number fours. They can be very good builders, farmers, miners or financial advisors and bankers. They may also be drawn towards work involving campaigning.

Lucky Colour: Green

Famous No.4's:
Arnold Schwarzenegger, Demi Moore, Clint Eastwood, John Major, Margaret Thatcher.

THE No.5 PERSON
Keith Duffy

Strengths:
Number five is the symbol of vitality and life. Fives tend to be clear thinkers, fast workers and full of enthusiasm. They are witty, competitive, friendly, passionate, magnetic and popular. They are daring and will try anything new. They love freedom and adventure. They have a passion for travel.

Weaknesses:
They can be unfocused, restless and indecisive. They often fear getting too close to one person. They can let their popularity bring them to fame and fortune yet never be self-fulfilled. They can also be demanding, deceitful and destructive.

Career Choices:
Number fives make great writers, salesmen, musicians, actors, scientists and researchers.

Lucky Colour: Blue

Famous No.5's:
Keith Duffy, Claudia Schiffer, Mick Jagger, André Agassi, Marlon Brando, Adolf Hitler.

THE No.6 PERSON
Mikey Graham & Shane Lynch

Strengths:
Six represents wisdom, harmony and the love of beauty and colour. They can be generous, loving, creative and compassionate. They are steady, patient and graceful. They often have high principles. They seek meaningful relationships and are very family oriented.

Weaknesses:
They can be argumentative, impractical and too idealistic. Sometimes they can be interfering and conceited.

Career Choices:
These are the wise carers of numerology. They are often drawn to careers in teaching, nursing, social work, gardening or farming. Sixes are always happy in occupations that make life or the environment more beautiful.

Lucky Colour: Gold

Famous No.6's:
Mikey Graham, Shane Lynch, Steven Spielberg, Meryl Streep, Stevie Wonder.

THE No.7 PERSON
Steve Gately

Strengths:
The number seven represents spirituality and mysticism. Sevens are thinkers. They are sensitive, perceptive and very spiritual. They are often modest, truthful and wise. They are very good at giving advice. They tend to be observant, loyal and have a great love of animals and nature.

Weaknesses:
They can be loners and introverts, and may appear emotionally cold and secretive. If they ignore their spiritual side they can become overindulgent, perhaps with food or drink.

Career Choices:
These perfectionists make very good artists, scientists, engineers and lawyers. Jobs that involve public service often appeal more than jobs that make money.

Lucky Colour: Pink

Famous No.7's:
Steve Gately, Diana, Princess of Wales, Elle McPherson, Marilyn Monroe, John F Kennedy, Winston Churchill.

THE No.8 PERSON

Strengths:
Number eight is the symbol of hard work and connections. Number eights are ambitious and energetic organisers. They have business flair, intelligence, confidence and determination. They have leadership qualities and are logical thinkers.

Weaknesses:
Eights can be proud, stubborn and unforgiving. They can also be very materialistic and greedy. Some eights can abuse power and can be ruthless, impatient, snappy and immoral.

Career Choices:
These organisers are ideal for careers in science, finance, supervising, law, the army and the police.

Lucky Colour: Navy

Famous No.8's:
Elizabeth Taylor, Joan Collins, Barbra Streisand, Neil Armstrong and Saddam Hussein.

THE No.9 PERSON

Strengths:
Number nine is the symbol of law and balance. It's also a sign of completion and perfection. Number nine people tend to be dutiful, self-controlled, broad-minded leaders. They love harmony and balance and are sharing, caring, happy people.

Weaknesses
They may be selfish and bossy. If their lives lack the balance they like, they can become aggressive, destructive and critical. They can also be vain and power hungry.

Career Choices:
These far-seeing visionaries make ideal teachers, preachers, surgeons and artists. Any job that improves the world and involves travel appeals to number nines.

Lucky Colour: White

Famous No.9's:
Dustin Hoffman, General Franco, Shirley MacLaine.

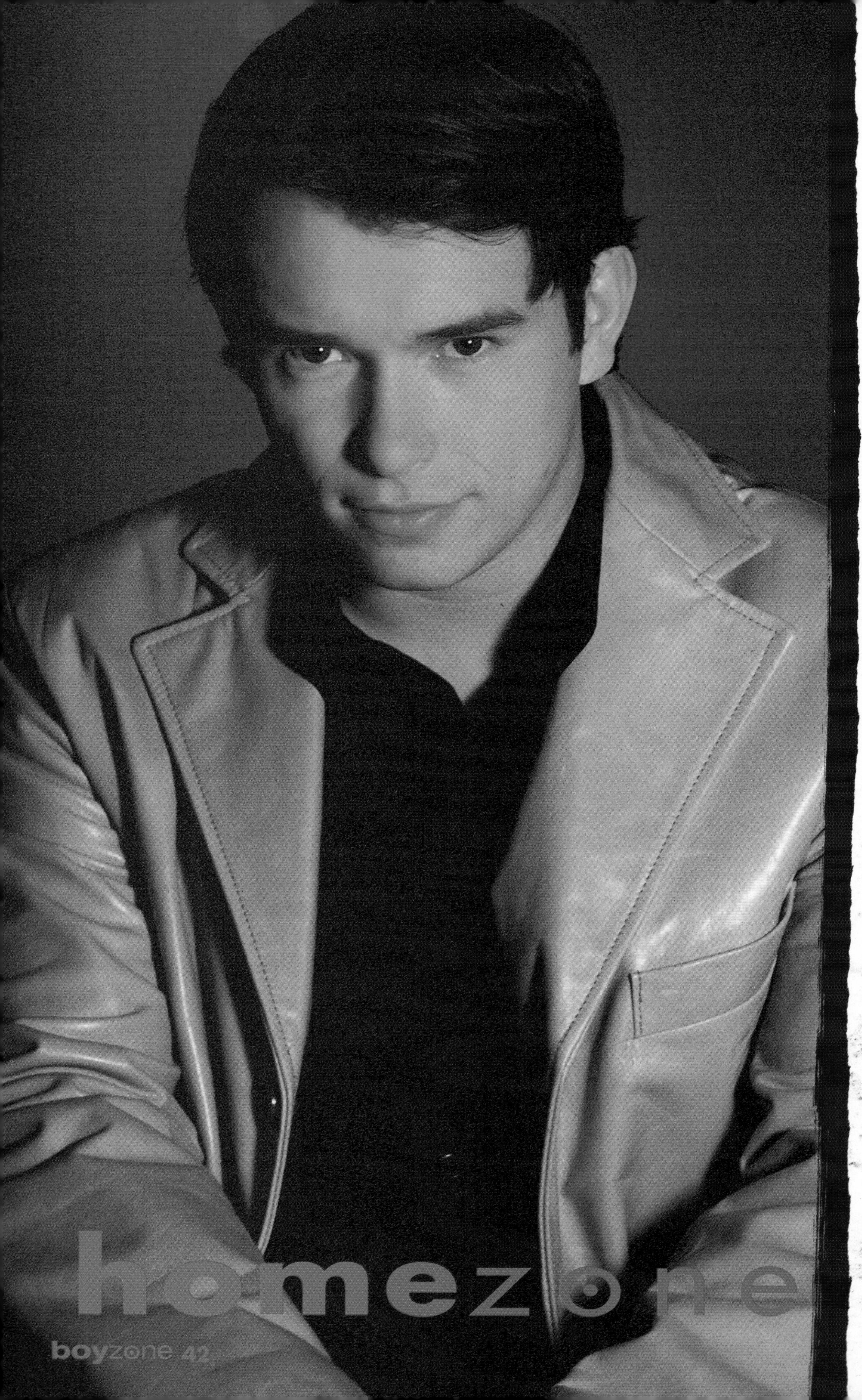
homezone

Steve

If you really want to get to know someone, you have to live with them. So who knows Steve better than his family?

Steve has three brothers: Mark (27), Alan (23) and Tony (16) and a sister, Michelle (25). Steve lives most of the time with Michelle and her husband and their baby Jordan in their family home. Here, Michelle spills the beanz on her little brother.

What was it like growing up with Steve?
We got on so well. He was very quiet, very content and lovable. He wasn't like my other brothers who used to spend their time pulling the head off my Barbie or flushing her down the toilet. He was a shy and sensitive child.

Who is Steve closest to in the family?
I think we're the closest. We were always close even as children. I'm his secretary and he lives with us and spoils his nephew Jordan something terrible. He's Jordan's godfather.

Did you fight a lot as kids?
No. We always got on well. We never row. Just once I remember having a row with him and two minutes later I was on the phone to him feeling so sorry for what I said.

Did he like school?
I think he did because his teachers doted on

him. He was a gorgeous child. My younger brother goes to the same school and they still ask after him and say if he's half as good as Steve he'll be fine. He was a dote.

Is he a mammy's boy or a daddy's boy?
He adores my mother, no doubt about it, but I'd never call him a mammy's boy. He's too independent for that.

Who did Steve share a room with?
When we were very young and lived in a flat, we all shared the same room. When we got older and moved to a house, I had my own room and all the boys shared.

Was he a tidy person?
He has always been very, very tidy.

Did you ever think he'd be famous?
He always set his mind on things and went for it. He joined drama classes not because my mother brought him there, he decided himself he was going. When he was going for Boyzone and he really wanted the part, I kept saying it didn't matter if he got it or not. I was just afraid of him getting hurt. I didn't want him to be let down so I suppose I didn't believe he'd be famous.

How often do you talk?
We talk every single day. Anytime he's away he calls. If he's home he usually lives with me most of the time. I leave long messages on his phone if I can't find him. I'd have a full conversation on the answering machine. He does the same – telling me what he's been up to all day, sometimes ten minutes long or more.

What interests do you share?
When we were kids it was always *Top of the Pops* on a Thursday night. We sat down to it religiously every week. Now we like the same books, we've the same taste in clothes and music. There's very little we don't agree about. I have some great brothers but he's the best brother anyone could ever have.

Keith

Personally Speaking

boyzone 44

You lead a crazy lifestyle in Boyzone. How do you stay sane?
Well, I think that's all down to my family. When I'm not working with Boyzone I lead an ordinary lifestyle at home and it helps to keep my feet firmly on the ground. Having little Jordan around is also a big help.

What's the best thing about being in Boyzone?
Having the power to make people happy. That's the best thing. Watching people smile and laugh when you're performing on stage and knowing that you have the power to do that is a wonderful feeling. As I've often said, for me that's what being in a pop group is all about.

What has been the best thing that's happened to you in your life?
My little son, Jordan. Like all dads, I bore people silly about him. But I've never known so much love. It's just a fantastic feeling having a little person who is your child and who absolutely adores you.

Are you a good dad?
I think so, but I do realise I've had the best of both worlds. I was away working with Boyzone and missed out on a lot of the work that goes with looking after a new baby. The way I look at it, I was providing for his future. When I'm home I give him all the attention he needs. I love him to bits, more than anything in the world.

Are you a good cook at home?
You must be joking! I'm a complete disaster. I couldn't boil an egg if me life depended on it. I've never cooked in me life.

Do you think Boyzone has helped you to develop as a person?
Absolutely. It has given me tremendous confidence because I used to be so insecure. People are always surprised when I say that because they thought I'd be cocky. But I didn't have an awful lot of confidence, even where girls were concerned. Achieving success with Boyzone gave me confidence to get through life. Now I really enjoy living because I know where I'm going.

Did you have a happy childhood?
I had a very happy home life, but I hated school, particularly at one secondary school. I was bullied all the time, which people might find strange because I'm such a big fella. Nobody liked me at the school and I was really depressed. I thought I had no good points. But then I moved to another school and made some great friends and I was a lot happier.

You have a dream life. Are you ever in a sad mood?
Sometimes. It is a fantastic trip being in Boyzone, but there are sacrifices as well. I miss me little son Jordan like mad when I'm away. It was really hard in the beginning when he came along because I had to go away for long periods and he wouldn't recognise me when I'd come home. That hurt bad.

Do you find it hard to go back to a normal life after you've been on tour with Boyzone?
It's really hard. You're out there playing to 30,000 screaming fans every night and being treated like a king, and it does take time to come back down and live a normal life at home.

What will you do after Boyzone?
I'd love a career in television, maybe presenting music shows or something like that. That would be really cool. Hopefully, I might even do some acting. I really do believe I have more to offer and having been a member of Boyzone will help to open doors for me.

Did you know?

Ronan

- **ONE** of Ronan's earlier ambitions was to become a policeman.

- **BEFORE** he joined the band, Ronan couldn't swim. But the other Boyz taught him in swimming pools at hotels where the group stayed on tour.

- **RONAN** reckons Shane is the sexiest member of Boyzone.

- **RONAN** hates smoking ever since he tried it at age 15 and it made him sick.

- **RONAN'S** biggest regret is once admitting that he was a virgin, because now it's a question he's always asked in interviews.

- **RONAN** has recorded a song with a turkey called Dustin. The turkey is a star on Irish TV and came from the same place as Zig and Zag. Ronan joined Dustin in a rendition of The Beatles' 'With A Little Help From My Friends' for the turkey's '97 Christmas album, called 'Faith Of Our Feathers'.

- **RONAN** prefers shopping in London and New York to his native Dublin. It's not as easy to get around in his own city because it's so small and fans find it easier to spot him.

Keith

- **WHEN** he was six or seven years old, Keith found a pair of scissors in the bathroom of his home and proceeded to cut triangles out of everything around the house. Needless to say, his parents were not impressed!

- **KEITH** loves cars and taught himself to drive. His first one was an Escort RS Turbo. "It was a beautiful car. It was blue," he recalls.

- **KEITH'S** first job was selling four-stone bags of potatoes on the roadside when he was eight or nine. He was paid £5 for his day's work…it was a small fortune to him at the time.

- **KEITH** once had a job as one of the security staff at concerts in Ireland. While guarding an after-show party for Peter Gabriel, he stopped Johnny Depp from entering because he didn't recognise the actor straight off.

- **KEITH** once went skinny dipping on his hols in Greece. But he didn't plan it. Two of his pals whipped off his trunks while they were in the sea and he had to stay in the water for ages!

Steve

• **STEVE** achieved a life-long ambition when he sang his song 'Shooting Star' on the soundtrack of the Disney animation movie *Hercules*.

• '**COLOURS** Of The Wind' from *Pocahontas* is Steve's favourite song from a Disney movie.

• **THE** first time Steve got really drunk was on his 21st birthday when the Boyz were in Argentina. He was ill for two days afterwards, poor soul. He insists it'll never happen again.

• **STEVE'S** first job was working in a bar when he was only 13. He admits he told a white lie about his age.

• **AS** a kid, Steve never had a family holiday.

• **ONE** of Steve's proudest moments was singing the *Hercules* song, 'Shooting Star', live at the premiere in London's Leicester Square.

Shane

- **SHANE'S** gold chain and bracelet cost him a whopping £10,000. He had them personally made just for him. Naturally, he loves them.

- **SHANE** likes baggy trousers and was very unhappy when he had to wear a Mr Bean-type tweed suit in the 'Picture Of You' video.

- **SHANE** gets in a funny mood when there's a full moon, and has to drink loads of water to stay normal.

- **SHANE** wants a job in the motor-racing business after Boyzone, preferably as a driver himself.

- **SHANE** collects tropical fish. He's got three scavenger fish, two sucker fish and two angel fish.

Mikey

• **MIKEY** is the oldest member of Boyzone, but he insists he still feels like he's only 18.

• **MIKEY** was not in the original line-up of Boyzone, which started out as a six-piece band. Two members were later dropped and Mikey was added to the group. Lucky chap.

• **THE** first famous group Mikey remembers meeting is the Bee Gees.

• **WHEN** he was a kid, Mikey got into trouble when he threw a firecracker in the fire of his family's living room, causing a massive explosion which covered the whole place in soot!

• **MIKEY** has problems sleeping and wakes up several times during the night. As a result, he's always tired during the day.

• **THE BOYZ** once dressed up as the Spice Girls on BBC 1's *Live And Kicking* show and surprised the real Spice Girls who were also on the show.

Steve

Personally Speaking

boyzone 50

What has been your biggest thrill?

There have been so many since I joined Boyzone. But I guess being involved with Disney has been the best thing ever.

What does being in a pop band mean to you?

I guess it's about bringing joy to people, creating good songs and music, putting on shows that are really spectacular and performing around the world.

Do you ever feel you're getting too old to be a pop star?

Absolutely no way. I still feel like I'm a teenager. There's some people in this business who've been doing it for forty years, so I've got a long way to go.

Have you ever thought of quitting Boyzone?

Sometimes, but only for a few minutes. People don't realise how hard it can be sometimes, trying to keep up with a really fast pace of living. It can really grind you down and you feel you want to be just doing a normal job. But it only lasts for a minute or two and then it's back to business.

Do you live it up in the clubs and trendy spots?

No, I'm not a party person at all. I'm usually so tired I just fall into bed and sleep. Anyway, I prefer to read a book or watch a movie.

Do you still worry about your looks?

Oh yeah, I'm never happy with the way I look. I don't look in the mirror and see somebody wonderful. I just see so many flaws. This year I tried to cut down on the amount of rubbish I eat.

Do you ever think about settling down?

To be honest, it would be just impossible while Boyzone continues to be a major part of my life. There is just no time for a personal life when you're in a hard-working pop band. But I have no regrets, I love every minute of Boyzone. Long may it continue, I say. So please keep on supporting us and make me happy.

Now that you're a pop star, do you feel you're different in any way?

No, not at all. My life is different, obviously. I'm very busy all the time and I get to travel the world. But as a person, I'm still the same Stephen Gately that my family and friends always knew. I probably have a bit more confidence now that I've achieved something. But I think that's natural – most people are like that when they get a job and start moving up in the world.

Do you have a bad temper?

I very seldom lose my temper. Hardly ever. Anyway, there's no point, 'cause people don't take me seriously. They just laugh at me. Honestly. It's enough to make you lose your temper.

Do you still suffer from pre-show nerves?

Yeah, I don't think the nerves will ever go away. They'll always be there.

What's your favourite part of being a pop star?

I like the fact that I can cheer people up with a little note or an autograph or a phone call or whatever. I hope if I was sad that people would do the same for me.

homezone

Ronan

If you really want to get to know someone, you have to live with them. So who knows Ronan better than his family?

Ronan has one sister, Linda, and three brothers, Kieran, Gerard and Gary. We talked to Ronan's eldest brother, Kieran. Kieran Keating is twelve years older than Ronan and also works in the music industry as road manager to The Carter Twins. Kieran revealed all.

What was Ronan like growing up at home?
He was very quiet. He was a really good kid. Because he was much younger than the rest of us – the second youngest, Gary, was six years older than him – everyone looked after him. He was pampered.

Did you and Ronan fight a lot?
No. He was too small to fight with. I think he and Gary got into a few fights though.

Was he a telltale?
No. I don't ever remember him telling tales.

Can you remember his favourite toy?
He lived on his BMX bicycle so I suppose that was his favourite.

Did he like school?
No. He preferred running and football. He was a very good little athlete. He won an All Ireland under 16s championship for sprinting one year.

Was he a mammy's boy or a daddy's boy?
He was definitely a mammy's boy. He was the baby and mam's favourite.

Do you remember when he was born?
Yes. I was twelve years old and he was born at home. I was in bed sick with a fever so I couldn't see him until he was three or four days old because we were afraid he would catch it too.

Did you have a nickname for him?
He'll probably kill me for this. We used to call him Tin Tin. He looked like a cartoon character that used to be on the telly at that time. He had tight hair which stuck up at the front. We all call him 'Ro' now.

Who did he share a room with?
He always shared with Gary. To this day they are very close. I think he's closer to Gary than anyone else. They have something very special.

Was he tidy?
He was then. But lately he's not. You'd want to see the state of his room at the moment.

What interests do you share with Ronan?
Music and cars. We like all the same singers – Sting and George Michael. Also I worked as a mechanic for years and was involved with a racing team. He was always mad into cars and motorbikes too. I brought a motorbike back from America after I'd been working there for five years. He went mad for it.

Did you ever think he'd be famous?
I don't think we ever think about our brothers or sisters being famous. Even now, sometimes we find it hard to believe what our Ro has done.

Know your Boyz

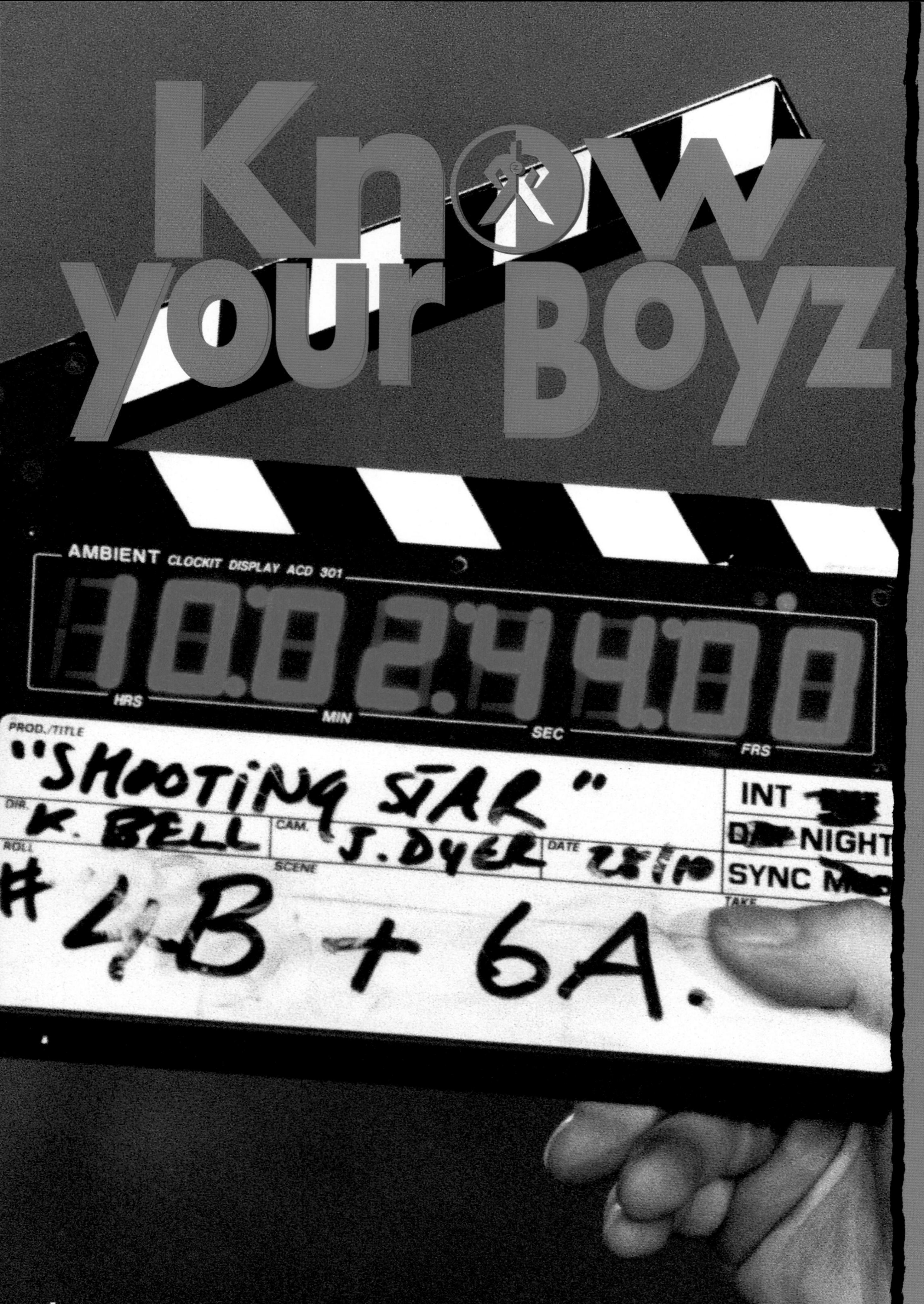
AMBIENT CLOCKIT DISPLAY ACD 301
10.02.44.00
HRS
MIN
SEC
FRS
PROD./TITLE
"SHOOTING STAR"
DIR.
K. BELL
CAM.
J. DYER
ROLL
DATE
28/10
SCENE
INT
NIGHT
SYNC
TAKE
#4B + 6A.

1. Which member of Boyzone had a pineapple hairdo?

2. Who are the two most fashion-conscious members of Boyzone?

3. Who is the least fashion-conscious member of Boyzone?

4. Which two members of Boyzone own Harley Davidson motorbikes?

5. Which member of Boyzone sang 'Shooting Star' in the Disney movie, *Hercules*?

6. Who is recognised as the leader of Boyzone?

7. Which two members of Boyzone are dads?

8. Which member of Boyzone is not associated with any organised religion?

9. Who is the editor of the official Boyzone magazine?

10. With which group did Boyzone's official photographer, Philip Ollerenshaw, once work?

11. Who has written the official books, *Boyzone In Person* and *Boyzone Living The Dream*?

12. What is the title of Boyzone's first hit?

13. With which French group did they later record it?

14. Boyzone's boss, Louis Walsh, once managed two Eurovision winners. Can you name them?

15. How many members were in the original Boyzone group?

16. What are Stephen's three favourite Disney movies?

17. Who pipped Boyzone's 'Father And Son' for the Christmas number one in '95?

18. Which member of Boyzone asks his mother to cut his toe nails?

19. Who sang lead vocals on Boyzone's first single, 'Working My Way Back To You'?

20. Which member of Boyzone was offered a place in the group after being spotted dancing in a nightclub?

ANSWERS: 1. Shane. 2. Ronan and Shane. 3. Mikey. 4. Ronan and Mikey. 5. Steve. 6. Ronan. 7. Keith and Mikey. 8. Shane. 9. Allison Maund. 10. Take That. 11. Eddie Rowley. 12. Working My Way Back To You. 13. Alliage. 14. Johnny Logan and Linda Martin. 15. Six. 16. Hercules, Sword in The Stone, Robin Hood. 17. Michael Jackson with Earth Song. 18. Keith. 19. Steve and Mikey. 20. Keith.

Mikey

MIKEY GRAHAM

PLACE OF BIRTH: **DUBLIN**

DATE OF BIRTH: **15.8.72**

STAR SIGN: **LEO**

HEIGHT: **5'8"**

COLOUR OF EYES: **BLUE**

STATUS:
A DAD - HIS DAUGHTER'S NAME IS HANNAH

FAVOURITE ACTOR:
ROBERT DE NIRO

FAVOURITE FOOD:
CHINESE

AMBITION:
TO BE A SOLO ROCK STAR AFTER BOYZONE

homezone

Shane

If you want to really know someone, you have to live with them. So who could tell us more about Shane than his family?

Shane has six sisters: Tara, Alison, twins Keavy and Edels, and Naomi. Shane's eldest sister, Tara (who is three years older than him), spilled the beanz on Shane. Tara is a singer with a new girlband called Fab.

What was he like as a brother growing up?
He was very quiet. He worked on his motorbike, his BMX and his skateboards all the time.

Did you fight a lot?
I don't think anyone really fought with him. He lived in the garage with his bikes. We never really saw him.

Was he a telltale?
No, never. He covered up for us most of the time. We used to write each other sick notes for school. We were very good at forging our mother's handwriting.

What is your earliest memory of him?
I remember him in the pram. We would be out racing the pram against other kids' prams.

What was his favourite toy when he was young?
He was really into all the *Star Wars* stuff.

Did you ever think he'd be famous?
No, not at all. He was always the type of person who kept to himself. He only went to the auditions for Boyzone because a friend of his, Mark Walton, was going.

What did he want to be when he grew up?
A racing driver. He still does. I don't think he's ever wanted to be anything else.

Was there any rivalry growing up?
No. There's none really between any of us. We're all very close.

Was he a mammy's boy or a daddy's boy?
I think he was equally close to both of them. I still think he talks to both of them together rather than one of them in particular.

Who did he share a room with?
None. He was the only boy so he got a room to himself. All us girls were thrown in together on top of each other while he lorded it in his own room.

Was he tidy?
He was real tidy. He had everything in its place and if we touched anything he'd kill us.

Who is he closest to in the family?
Probably Alison. They're very close in age – she's only a year older than him. She's also into racing cars and the sort of thing that Shane is really into.